PAELLA

PAELLA

ALBERTO HERRAIZ

ALL ABOUT PAELLA

Most of us have eaten paella at least once, and we think we know it well because it has become very familiar. But there is a lot more to it than we think. Unquestionably, the most important element of the culture of paella is its festive dimension. The expression *ir de paella*, 'to go for a paella', has become synonymous in colloquial Spanish with 'to have fun'. It literally means 'to go to a particular place in order to cook a paella'. This would usually be at the weekend, in the open air, at a house in the countryside. The paella would be cooked over a *paellero*, a type of barbecue designed especially for cooking the dish; paella may also be cooked over a campfire. Traditionally, on such occasions men take charge of everything, from the fire to the cooking, combining a true food-lover's attitude to relaxation and conviviality with the head of the household's responsibilities on the customary day of rest. Considerable prestige is attached to this Sunday dish, and the ceremony of its preparation is full of tradition. Outdoors the *paellero* (the term is also used to describe the man who cooks the paella) is in charge. Indoors, however, in the kitchen, it is the *paellera* – the woman – who makes the preparations.

My aim in this book is to provide the reader with much more than a mere collection of recipes. The real objective is to explain paella as a culinary technique and show its practical applications in the form of recipes. Italian risotto obeys the same principles, in that it is a simple technique that can be adapted, resulting in limitless variations on a basic theme.

As a cook, the most important thing for me is to simplify the techniques used for making paella, without compromising the authenticity of the finished dish or its essential appeal. My aim is to make paella universal so that anyone, anywhere, can prepare it. I have tried to bring it up to date and develop it further without betraying its traditional character. 'Foodies', in my opinion, are often too fixated on the concept of the original and authentic recipe. However, in times gone by there were no written recipes at all. They were passed on orally, through demonstration and example. Dishes evolved over time, just as I am enabling paella to evolve through my creation of new varieties such as 'white' paellas, in which the *sofrito* (a basic preparation of tomatoes cooked with garlic and onions) and saffron are replaced by ingredients borrowed from other culinary traditions, and even sweet paellas for dessert. And why not?

Opposite: Majorcan 'Dirty' Paella Rice
(page 158)

PAELLA AND ME

A NATIONAL DISH

There is no firm date for the invention of paella. Written evidence of its existence started to appear around the eighteenth century and became more frequent during the nineteenth century. This was probably connected with the development of local metalwork industries and improvements in steel-making techniques that allowed for mass production, which in turn made more sophisticated carbon steel cooking pans more affordable and available to a wider public. Cooked in such pans, paella very quickly became a popular dish. As time went by, it became synonymous with Spanish cuisine. This trend increased in the years following World War II, reflecting the development of tourism in Spain.

Rice plays an important role in Spanish cooking. It arrived on the Iberian peninsula via Persia, where it had been cultivated for centuries, and was probably first introduced in Andalusia, in the south, brought by the Moors who settled there in the eighth century. As time went by, Moorish culture and the use of rice spread northwards and the cooking methods changed. It was in Valencia, eastern Spain, that paella as we now know it was created.

In Valencia, paella is associated with Sundays and feast days. Elsewhere 'paella day' varies: in Catalonia, and particularly in Barcelona, Thursday sees its appearance on the menus of neighbourhood restaurants, bars and unpretentious eating places. Strictly speaking, the name 'paella' only applies to the Valencian version. It is not correct to call other versions of the dish 'paella'; instead they are known as *arroz en paella*, which literally means 'rice cooked in a paella pan'. In this book I have used the term 'paella rice' to describe the recipes.

In Spain, a recipe for paella is an ancestral legacy passed down from generation to generation. As with all traditional dishes, there is a great deal of inherited knowledge involved. Each generation of cooks follows the same procedures instinctively. The way the vegetables are prepared, the right time to add the stock, the choice of seasonings: none of these things hold any mystery for them. While respecting the history of the cooks from whom I have inherited these traditions, my task is to explore and describe everything connected with paella for those who do not have this culinary inheritance.

A RICE REVOLUTION

Over the years my research has resulted in a minor culinary revolution when it comes to paella rice. Once I started thinking about rice, I began to question everything I thought I knew about it. I literally had to re-learn how to cook paella. My first step was to eat in Spain's best restaurants, so that I could take what I learned from these meals and use it to formulate a system of precise timing and a consistent technique. Next, I tried to incorporate the best and most useful innovations and techniques of contemporary cooking within this system. I knew that I had to use only the best ingredients including rice, flavourings and oil.

Opposite: Paella Rice with Lobster
(page 142)

One day in Rome, I was served a *pizza bianca* (a pizza without any tomato). This set me thinking. Why not make a *paella blanca*? With this in mind, I left out the tomatoes when I next made a paella, resulting in an infinitely adaptable dish that could be made with basic ingredients from all over the world. I did not create this white paella for health reasons. My aim was to find a new combination of ingredients to flavour the rice. This spirit of experimentation also led to the creation of my 'fusion' paellas, in which a recipe from one country interacts with ingredients from another. I remain true to the basic principles of paella, while adding ingredients from elsewhere. This has led to such innovations as my recipes for 'Return to India' Paella Rice (page 122) and my 'Return to Colombo' Paella Rice with Lobster (page 110), to give just two examples.

Deconstructing the basic paella techniques meant that I had to gain some distance from my native culture – I had to leave Spain. This is why I live in Paris. This city has enabled me to appreciate the value of precision and refinement in cooking and has enabled me to make the world of paella accessible to everyone.

A SPANIARD IN PARIS

I was born in Cuenca, in the province of Castilla-La Mancha in central Spain; I belong to the fifth generation of a family of chefs and restaurant owners. I was surrounded by experts when it came to Spanish culinary traditions. Over the past ten years and more, the cooking of the Iberian peninsula has captured the attention of the whole world: not for its traditional cuisine, but because of its adventurous chefs and their contemporary creations. This curiosity works both ways. The world watches Spain, while in Spain the culinary world looks outwards. For me it works slightly differently: as a Spanish cook who has settled in Paris, I always look to my native land for inspiration. I study Spain, I think about Spain; I try to present my country's cuisine in a contemporary and subtle way. Meanwhile, my interpretation of Spanish cooking is influenced by my chosen vantage point in Paris.

ONE RESTAURANT, ONE SPECIALITY

My restaurant in Paris, Fogón, first opened in 1997. Nowadays it can be found beside the Seine, on the rue des Grands-Augustins, but originally it was situated between Saint-Julien-le-Pauvre Church (the city's oldest church) and Notre-Dame Cathedral. For me, coming to work in Paris after having been in charge of Mesón Nella (the family restaurant in Cuenca) following my mother's death, felt like being at the centre of things. Paris, its inhabitants and its culture have always attracted me far more strongly than France itself. I have established myself in what I consider to be the cradle of a unique, highly cultivated cuisine, codified by the great French chefs Escoffier and Carême.

Since I came to live in the Paris of my dreams, I felt that I had to offer the city something in exchange. Once I had completed my market research, I decided to open a restaurant based on a single speciality, paella, which at that time was an unknown concept in Paris. In practice there were two specialities: paella and tapas. Why did I choose these two? Primarily because these are the best known and the least well understood of all Spanish dishes. I wanted not only to offer the best, but also to make my clientele forget paella as they thought they knew it – the paella one encounters all too often outside Spain, in mass catering, in canteens (cafeterias) or as a ready-made meal on supermarket shelves. I call these 'impossible paellas'. They sometimes have a pleasant flavour but are bland, and the individual taste of each ingredient has been lost. The rice is merely a background, unlike the authentic paellas that Spanish people truly appreciate, where it is the rice itself that really counts.

The symbolic starting point of a paella is a fire – Fogón means 'hearth', and shares the associated connotations. But open fires are not feasible in Parisian restaurants. I therefore decided to complete the cooking of my paellas in the oven. This solution, which initially might have seemed frustrating, turned out to be a blessing. Cooking in the oven has many advantages. The paella cooks evenly, facilitating an interesting variation in textures, and the starch in the rice comes to the surface and forms a crust. It has taken fourteen years' work to perfect this texture.

UTENSILS

A PAN WITH TWO HANDLES

First and foremost, the word 'paella' denotes an object: the pan in which it is cooked. Secondly, it is a method of preparation that takes its name from this utensil. Something similar has occurred with the tagines of Morocco and the *tians* of Provence – both are cooking vessels after which dishes have been named.

Paella pans are used in Catalonia, in the Levante (the central-eastern region of Spain) and in the Balearic Islands, but nowhere more so than in Valencia. The traditional paella pan, made from polished carbon steel, is round in shape with low, slanting sides that curl over slightly around the edge, and has two curved handles set diametrically opposite one another, each one attached to the side with two rivets. Depending on the region, some pans have straight sides, without a lip, and they can vary in depth.

The metal used for making the paella pan is always thin because it must transmit heat immediately and also cool quickly when the heat source is turned off. Heat control is very important when making paella. The diameter of the utensil depends on how many people are to be served (individual paella pans do not exist). The bottom of the pan is not flat but slightly concave, and marked all over its surface with tiny, shallow dimples, which help to maintain the curve of the metal bottom. I exploit this concave shape fully because it enables me to vary the texture of the rice.

There are, however, other types of paella pan. Each has its advantages and its drawbacks. Whichever type you choose, make sure that it fits inside your oven!

POLISHED, CARBON STEEL PAELLA PANS

These are the classic traditional pans. They are inexpensive and provide the best results. One of their advantages is that they develop a patina through being used time after time. This patina is caused by oxidation and is the result of a reaction with ingredients such as artichokes, Swiss chard, spinach and aubergines (eggplant), turning the rice a dark, greenish-grey colour and giving it a slightly metallic taste, which can seem strange to some people but is appreciated by connoisseurs of paella. I like to compare it to mature red wines made from Cabernet Sauvignon grapes, which also develop this metallic flavour as they age.

Because polished, carbon steel paella pans have this tendency to oxidation, it is necessary to look after them to prevent them from rusting. Immediately after purchase, the pan should be cleaned and prepared for use. To do this, keep dipping a cloth in white wine vinegar as you rub the metal with it, thereby removing the protective varnish applied in the factory. Fill the paella pan with soapy water, add a generous handful of coarse salt and boil for 5 minutes. Empty the paella pan and rinse it well. Dry it with a clean cloth. Using another clean, dry cloth, coat the pan with a little olive oil. Wash the paella pan each time you use it – you can use dish-washing liquid – dry it and oil it again. If the pan is not used for a while, the protective coating of oil will turn rancid. If this happens, wash the pan before using it again. The concave bottom of this type of paella pan makes it unsuitable for use on solid electric and ceramic stoves or cooktops, as well as Aga stoves or similar cooking ranges.

ENAMELLED STEEL PAELLA PANS

These are just as traditional as the previous type and easier to look after. They are, however, much less robust because the enamel coating tends to chip easily. Being made from a material that is not very durable, they must not be banged or handled roughly. If the enamel is damaged, the chipped surface must be cleaned, then oiled. This type of paella pan is, however, suitable for use with all heat sources.

STAINLESS STEEL PAELLA PANS

These have the same characteristics as polished, carbon steel paella pans, but do not need oiling between uses – just washing and drying. They do not, however, develop the oxidation patina that imparts such a unique taste to the paella.

REINFORCED STAINLESS STEEL PAELLA PANS

Stainless steel pans are also available with thicker, reinforced bottoms that are completely flat and suitable for all kinds of heat sources, including induction stoves. The thick bottom conducts the heat more slowly, so some of the responsiveness to heat that is characteristic of traditional paella pans is lost. They also retain the heat for longer after cooking. This is the type of pan I would recommend if you do not have an oven, because it can be placed on two or three hot plates at the same time.

A polished, carbon steel paella pan

A non-stick paella pan (outside) and a stainless steel paella pan with reinforced bottom (inside)

An enamelled steel paella pan

stainless steel paella pan

A cast iron paella pan

A sauté pan

CAST IRON PAELLA PANS

Heavier and more difficult to handle than the other paella pans, these do not permit efficient heat control or variations in the rice's texture, nor do they develop an oxidation patina in the same way as polished carbon steel. If you use this type of pan, allow for the lengthy heating time and for heat retention after the paella is cooked.

NON-STICK PAELLA PANS

These paella pans are available with or without a reinforced bottom such as a steel sandwich base. Their disadvantage is the fragility of the non-stick coating, which prohibits scraping the bottom of the pan with a metal spoon. They do have the advantage of allowing a *socarret* (crust) to form evenly, without sticking to the pan.

USING OTHER PANS TO MAKE PAELLA

You can always improvise by using other, similarly shaped utensils as paella pans, such as frying pans or skillets, casserole dishes, sauté pans, a wok, perhaps, or even a disposable aluminium foil container. Earthenware dishes and casseroles produce softer-textured rice, but it is difficult to control the heat. Remember that although the original polished, carbon steel paella pan is still the best, what really counts is the end result.

A SIMPLE RECIPE, A RANGE OF POSSIBILITIES

The basic constituents of paella are as follows: a cereal (usually rice) is cooked in a paella pan with a fish fumet or stock, seasonings and at least three or four main ingredients (meat, fish or seafood, vegetables), which are added to flavour the rice. It is important not to use too many ingredients, so that each individual taste can be appreciated and the whole dish is coherent.

Preparation starts with gently cooking a *sofrito* (usually garlic, onions and tomatoes), similar to the flavouring base of an Italian *soffritto* or a French *mirepoix*, which will combine with the liquid. Depending on how elaborate the paella is to be, finely ground pine nuts or almonds may be added during the cooking process. When the *sofrito* has cooked for just long enough, the rice is added and is heated and stirred until the grains are translucent, taking up the oil and flavourings. Finally, the stock is added and everything is cooked until all the liquid has evaporated. By the time this happens, each rice grain should have absorbed the flavour of all the other ingredients.

While it may be true that there are as many paella recipes as there are cooks, nevertheless several styles of paella can be identified, from the simplest to the most elaborate, from the everyday to the most festive. To start with, there is paella cooked in the kitchen and paella prepared on a barbecue or outdoor grill: the methods differ. For the kitchen version, the stock is prepared in advance and added during the cooking process. Over a barbecue or grill, the entire process takes place in the paella pan. Many of these different ways of preparing paella have traditionally been carried out using an earthenware cooking vessel.

TRADITIONAL PAELLA

The most traditional paella is *paella valenciana* (Valencian paella), which is the choice of paella purists. Valencia's paella has evolved around the rice that is cultivated in the region's Albufera marshes, enriched with local produce such as chicken, rabbit, vegetables, snails, eels, even game when in season. The rest is determined by the region's typical flavourings and seasonings: garlic, tomatoes, saffron, *pimentón* (Spanish smoked paprika), olive oil.

IMPROVISED PAELLAS

These are very much part of Spanish everyday life, and consist of a rice dish made with what is to hand. They begin with a careful assessment of what is left in the storecupboard (pantry), refrigerator or freezer, and anything is eligible for inclusion, such as seasonings, vegetables or canned ingredients.

PAELLA *A BANDA*

This is paella made with a fumet (concentrated stock) of rock fish and seafood that is strained after the fish or seafood has cooked in it. The term *a banda* means 'on the side', referring to the fact that the ingredients used to make the fumet are eaten separately while the rice is cooking. The rice is very flavoursome, which is the object of the exercise, but the fish used for the broth will have yielded all its flavour to the broth, leaving behind little more than fish bones for the diner. Traditionally, the fish is eaten before the rice, and the rice is then served on its own. At my restaurant, Fogón, we serve paella *a banda* without the *banda*.

PAELLA *BRUT*

This is best translated as 'coarse' or 'dirty', and refers to paellas containing many ingredients in their natural state, including seafood shells and bones. They require a lot of work at the table.

PAELLA *CIEGA*

Literally 'blind paella'. All the *banda* ingredients that are cooked with the rice have been carefully prepared (removing any bones or shells) so that they can be eaten just as they are. This type of paella can be eaten with your eyes shut because there is no risk of coming across a shell or a bone.

PAELLA *EN COSTRA*

Literally 'paella with an egg crust'. Beaten eggs are poured over the paella when it is nearly done. The recipe used is a *paella ciega* (see above), to which the beaten eggs are added, before the dish is then finished in the oven.

HOW TO MAKE PAELLA

WHAT YOU NEED TO KNOW

To make good paella, you must limit your choice of ingredients, otherwise the dish will be overloaded and will lack the specific flavours that make it unique. Each component of the paella should retain its individual character, while at the same time contributing to the unmistakable character of the whole dish. When selecting the ingredients for your paella it helps to know a little about seafood families: the cuttlefish, squid and octopus family, the prawn (shrimp) families, the langoustine family, the crayfish family. The flavours are transmitted through the fumet (fish stock), which imparts to the rice all the flavour of the ingredients.

UNITS OF MEASUREMENT AND TIMING

Measures of weight and volume can vary, depending on your heat source and the rate of evaporation it allows. You may have to adapt the information given in the recipes. The trick is to test them. If you find your paella is too dry, add a little more stock and make a note of this for the next time. If the paella is too moist, you can adjust the cooking time and the heat setting. These recipes are guides; in the final analysis, you will need to learn through experience how to handle your rice, your measurements and your timings.

Timing is very important when preparing paella and a kitchen timer or watch is a useful aid: allow 17 minutes from when the rice starts to boil in its stock. Remember that this is a real countdown. Once the stock has been added and the rice has started to cook, there must be no interruption, no matter what happens. You need a high heat to begin with, and this should be gradually reduced as the cooking process progresses towards its end. You must always watch your timings very carefully, and meticulously measure quantities. Once you have adjusted the timing as well as the quantities of rice, basic flavouring, oil and stock to your satisfaction, you can stick to this formula and be sure of successful paellas, no matter which recipe you have chosen.

SOFRITO

A *sofrito* is an aromatic mixture based on onions, garlic and tomatoes gently cooked in olive oil and used to add flavour to the rice and stock. This is the first stage in preparing a paella and must be done over low heat to prevent the mixture from burning or drying out: these details can have a huge effect on the taste of the finished dish. Adding a little stock to finish cooking the *sofrito* will prevent it from burning.

A traditional *sofrito* follows certain rules, which vary from region to region. In Alicante they like very highly flavoured *sofritos* in which ñora peppers play an important role. The purists of Valencia use grated fresh tomato as the main ingredient. In Barcelona both these methods are combined, with the addition of onions and, sometimes, a *picada* (a paste made of dried fruits, garlic and ñora peppers, pounded with other aromatics in a mortar with a pestle). Personally, I like all three; everything depends on the recipe.

Opposite: Paella Rice with Rabbit and Sna
(page 14

FRYING THE RICE

The first step in cooking the rice is to infuse it with flavoured oil, which helps to make it very tasty. The rice is added to the paella pan containing the *sofrito* and oil, and cooked gently while being stirred continuously, until the grains are translucent and coated in the oil (see photograph, page 29). At this point the liquid is added. I have done a lot of work on this process. It has advantages and disadvantages, the advantages being that flavours are released more readily in the presence of fats, and the rice tends to be less sticky once it's cooked. As for the disadvantages, it is very important to allow all the moisture to evaporate first, so that the rice absorbs only the oil, because as soon as rice comes into contact with water it starts to cook. It is therefore best not to prolong this stage and to add the stock as soon as possible. As soon as the rice becomes translucent and you can see the kernel or 'heart' of each grain, you must stop stirring it over the heat. If this stage lasts too long, the grains will revert to opaque white and be spoilt.

Some cooks omit this process when making paella: they cook the *sofrito*, then stir in hot stock before sprinkling in the rice, which results in a slightly different dish. This happens naturally when cooking paella outdoors, because in this case the stock is made in the paella pan instead of being added separately.

SOCARRET

The *socarret* is the layer of crunchy rice that forms on the bottom of the paella (see photograph, page 29). You can ensure that it forms whether you cook on gas, on the barbecue (grill) or over another heat source. It should be crunchy and stick to the bottom of the pan without becoming bitter or at all burnt. The *socarret* layer should also be thin – only as thick as a single rice grain. To produce it, place the paella pan over very high heat once the liquid has evaporated. The steam released has an agreeable aroma to begin with; as soon as it begins to smell slightly acrid, take the paella pan off the heat.

If the heat is not evenly distributed under the paella pan, keep shifting the pan to produce the *socarret*. The smell given off by the steam will be your guide. The *socarret* forms more readily in a pan with a reinforced bottom or, even better, in a non-stick pan, where it will caramelize without sticking, rather like a fritter.

When serving the paella, the *socarret* is placed alongside the soft rice. This practice of producing different rice textures in the same dish occurs elsewhere in the world. In China and Iran, for example, several methods are used to produce a highly valued crust on the bottom of the cooking pan.

PROPORTIONS AND TEXTURES

The size of the paella pan depends on how many people you are cooking for. Paella is never made for one person because the ingredients will not complement one another satisfactorily if the paella is too small. Size is also linked to the desired texture. If you want to serve an extra-fine, dual-textured paella for two people, you will need a 40-cm (15¾-inch) pan; a moister paella for the same number calls for a smaller pan (see the chart below). Size can also depend upon your ingredients. If you use cod, for example, which is a very gelatinous fish, the bottom layer will caramelize, even when you are cooking a moist paella.

This chart enables you to choose the size of paella pan according to the number of portions needed and the texture you want to achieve, although the intensity of your heat source also affects the latter. Of course, compromise is sometimes necessary, as you cannot buy every size of paella pan. Here are some basic proportions:

Number of guests	For a moist texture	For an extra-fine texture
2	Ø 34 cm (13½ inches)	Ø 41 cm (16 inches)
3	Ø 41 cm (16 inches)	Ø 47 cm (18½ inches)
4	Ø 47 cm (18½ inches)	Ø 51 cm (20 inches)
5	Ø 51 cm (20 inches)	Ø 55 cm (22 inches)
6	Ø 60 cm (24 inches)	Ø 64 cm (25 inches)

Paella is a sociable dish, but it is best not to cook it for too many people. Traditionally, eight servings is the maximum recommended number. Paellas are rarely cooked for more than ten people, despite the fact that giant versions are served nowadays at some large gatherings. For the best results, make a paella to yield anything from four to six portions, ideally six. When cooking for twelve people, it is best to make two separate paellas, each to serve six, rather than one large one: the larger the paella, the less precision can be achieved in the cooking.

INGREDIENTS

RICE

Rice is not an accompaniment to paella: it is the dish itself. In Spain the ingredients that are used to flavour it such as fish or seafood (the *banda*) play secondary roles: the expression *a banda* means 'on the side'. Sometimes the rice is even served without the *banda*, which is set aside, or only the rice is eaten and the *banda* is left on the plate: it is usually less flavoursome than the rice because its primary function is to release all its flavour into the rice.

The botanical species rice (*Oryza sativa*) is divided into two major subspecies: *indica* and *japonica*. *Indica* has long narrow grains and is usually served as an accompaniment because it does not absorb flavours readily. It does, however, have a pronounced flavour of its own (as in the case of Indian basmati rice and Thai jasmine rice). It can be successfully used for sweet dishes. *Japonica* has short oval grains. It has little flavour of its own, but forms an excellent vehicle for other flavours. The rice that is most suited to paellas belongs to this subspecies, which is popular throughout the Mediterranean.

Rice is classified into three distinct categories, depending on the average length of the grain: long-grain rice must be at least 6 mm long, medium-grain rice measures 5–6 mm (⅕–¼ inch), round- or short-grain rice is less than 5 mm (⅕ inch).

The main varieties of rice used for paella in Spain are senia, bomba, bahía and thaibonnet, all short-grain varieties. It is worth noting that Calasparra rice, a short-grain rice widely available outside Spain, is not a variety in itself, but instead a protected designation of origin, which means that it must traditionally be grown in a particular geographical area to be given this name. Various varieties of rice such as bomba, senia and so on can be awarded this designation. Bomba (see opposite, bottom right) is the most widely used and sought-after rice for paellas due to its exceptional capacity for absorbing liquid. It can absorb at least one-and-a-half times its own volume of water. Also, it keeps its shape as it cooks because it swells lengthwise, and this provides a useful margin for error in timing. The bomba rice plant is quite tall and not very productive, and the availability of the rice depends upon the success of the harvest. It almost entirely disappeared because of its low yield, but its cultivation has recently undergone a renaissance. Bomba rice-growing territory is divided into three or four protected designations of origin.

Despite the fact that this top-quality rice is three times as expensive as the other varieties, it is still good value for money. If you cannot buy bomba, Calasparra or another suitable Spanish rice, you can substitute other varieties of short-grain rice: Camargue, Japanese or Italian risotto rice such as arborio or carnaroli make suitable choices. Avoid 'quick-cook' parboiled or converted rice, which is unsuitable. And do not be tempted to use brown rice; it takes too long to cook. Regardless of the variety you choose, the rice must be of top quality, with no bits in it or broken grains. Damaged grains will release starch and make the rice sticky. The grains should be in perfect condition and uniform in colour. Although it is difficult for rice producers to ensure that 100 per cent of the grains are of the same variety, the rice you use should be as homogenous as possible. None of the grains should have brown or chalky-white stripes; they should not be dirty nor have a greenish or reddish tinge to them. Rice that has been affected by fermentation or insect infestation should be discarded, and no trace of the germ should remain. The rice should also have undergone the correct drying process after being harvested, and its moisture content should not exceed 15 per cent.

Milling is the process of preparing the rice grains for cooking, in which the first step is removing the husk, or outer skin, enclosing the rice grain. Depending on the method used, the whiteness of the rice will vary. In Spain, some old mills with millstones leave some of the husk on the rice, and there are also some modern mills that are designed to leave a little of it in place. This makes the rice slightly more flavoursome. The moment at which the grain has its husk removed and is further processed or polished is more important than the date of harvest, since rice can be stored for quite a long time if it has not had the husk removed. Once the husk has been removed, the rice should be used as soon as possible (this is particularly so with brown rice, which becomes rancid more quickly than white) or stored in a dry dark place.

Here are some tips for cooking rice. Never rinse it because this detracts from the texture of the finished dish. Do not mix varieties of rice or use rice from more than one package, even if they are the same type, because this can lead to uneven cooking. Measure

Pounding saffron (see page 24)

Preparing saffron for toasting (see page 52)

pimentón, or Spanish smoked paprika (see page 23)

Bomba paella rice (see page 20)

out the rice for your paella according to the number of portions: allow 100 g (½ cup) short-grain white rice per person.

To be successful with rice, you need to learn how to tell when it is perfectly cooked. To check, select a grain of cooked rice and cut it in half across the middle of the grain, then examine it (you could use a magnifying glass if you have one). You should no longer be able to distinguish the 'kernel', or heart of the grain, which should remain firm. If this kernel is still too obvious, the rice will be indigestible. The whole grain should burst and yield when it is bitten. Each grain should be separate from the rest. These are the keys to cooking perfect rice.

STOCKS AND FUMETS

Almost an entire chapter of this book is devoted to the stocks and fumets (see page 38) that are used to cook the rice in a paella. They must be made with the purest water. Tradition dictates that only water from Valencia makes a good paella, but this has no scientific basis. At home, use tap water if it is of good quality, or else mineral or filtered water. If your water is very hard and if you are making a stock with shellfish shells, add a few drops of white wine vinegar to reduce the hardness of the water. If you cook rice in water that is too hard (with too high a mineral content), you risk impairing the cooking process.

The amount of liquid you will need always depends on the quantity of rice, regardless of your chosen cooking method. You must also make allowances for the type of heat source on which you will be cooking the paella and always add very hot stock to ensure that boiling point is reached almost immediately. If the stock has not completely evaporated when the cooking time is up, allow it to evaporate by keeping the paella over high heat for a few minutes. If a lot of liquid remains, you will need to use a spoon to discard it. If you have followed the recipe carefully, however, this should not usually be the case – but accidents can always happen. If there is not enough liquid left and the rice is under-cooked, add a little more stock, but it must be boiling hot. If the rice is almost cooked, cover the entire surface of the paella with a clean, damp dish towel and prolong the cooking time by 2 minutes (see photograph, page 29). The important thing is never to interrupt the cooking of the rice once it is under way.

SALT

The recipes for stock included in this book are not salted. Salt should be added directly to the paella. Add it in moderation at the beginning, then taste the paella a little later and add a little more if needed. It is essential that all the salt be added before the rice has started to cook and swell to the extent that its volume exceeds that of the stock; after this point the seasoning cannot be adjusted. This point is usually reached 2–3 minutes after the liquid is added. Do not forget that the liquid concentrates as it evaporates, thus bringing out the taste of the salt, so always add this sparingly. You should also not forget that, even without added salt, some stocks have such an intense flavour that their strength can deceive you into thinking that they are salted. This is the case with Black Paella Rice with Cuttlefish Ink (page 74), the stock for which is very concentrated.

OIL

Olive oil is used for most paellas, but depending on the recipe other oils can be chosen, such as toasted sesame oil, groundnut (peanut) oil or sweet almond oil. Selecting the most appropriate type of oil when you first add the rice can only result in a more full-flavoured paella.

It is important to distinguish between mild or medium olive oil used for cooking – which does not need to be of the finest quality because it loses its flavouring properties once it has exceeded 80°C (176°F) – and extra-virgin olive oil used for flavouring. A few olive varieties, such as Cornicabra, produce oil that has a high smoke point (in other words, it can withstand high temperatures).

You can make your own flavoured oils (see page 58). I make garlic oil by steeping garlic cloves in olive oil for 3 months in a cold place. In France, where some people are a little wary of garlic, it is a good way of using this ingredient. I have also learned a lot from Ferran Adrià, the chef at Spain's celebrated elBulli restaurant. He was the source of inspiration for my Ibérico Ham-flavoured Oil (page 62). In order to impart the flavour of *pata negra* ham to rice, I cut off a little of the pink ham fat and let it steep in olive oil for 3 months in a cold store. The oil retains its colour, but also takes up the flavour of the ham.

Another method of flavouring oil is to steep the ingredients in it for 30 minutes in a microwave oven on the defrost setting. The oil is then left to cool, and you repeat the process once or twice. These short infusions are particularly suited to aromatic herbs. You can also flavour oils with all manner of products: dried fruit, plants used for seasoning, mushrooms, seafood shells. I also make a sardine oil using fried heads and bones. It is best to choose a neutral-flavoured oil such as rapeseed (canola), sunflower or grapeseed oil for this kind of short infusion because this will successfully absorb flavours. Olive oil, however, remains the best choice for long infusions.

PIMENTÓN

This bright red spice (see photograph, page 21) is often called 'Spanish paprika', which is not altogether accurate. Christoper Columbus brought back chillies and sweet peppers (*Capsicum annuum*) from the Americas, and presented them to the monks of a Spanish monastery to thank them for the help they had given him. From these specimens cultivation of the sweet pepper developed in the Spanish province of Cáceres, which eventually resulted in *pimentón* as we know it. Three varieties of long, pointed peppers are grown in order to produce Spanish paprika. The peppers are dried, sometimes smoked, and reduced to a powder and sifted. They can be ground in a millstone up to twelve times before the final sifting. Depending on the variety and the amount of peppers used, paprika can be more or less smoked, spicy, sweet or acidulated. Each producer has their own blend. Whether smoked or unsmoked paprika is used depends on the region: in La Vera, where the smoked variety is made, this is the preferred choice, while in Valencia the unsmoked variety is favoured. Apart from its aromatic and colouring properties, paprika acts as a natural preservative, particularly for cured meats.

SAFFRON

Saffron, which originates in the western Mediterranean (probably in Crete), is the world's most valuable spice by weight. It is an extract of the crocus flower (*Crocus sativus*), which lives only for a day. The stigmas are dried at 30–35°C (86–95°F) for 10–12 hours. A huge volume of flowers is needed to obtain a pinch of the red stigmas and stalks, and gathering saffron is a laborious manual exercise that yields little profit, and usually constitutes a second rather than a principal income. In Spain, the central region of La Mancha is where most saffron is produced.

Substitutes such as aromatic coloured powders are often used because saffron is so expensive. In Valencia they make a virtue of using these coloured powders instead of natural saffron. A few saffron threads are added for appearance's sake, but the difference in colour is very noticeable. The coloured powders produce a hue that verges on yellow, while real saffron veers towards orange.

There are a few rules to be observed when using saffron. The threads must not be added directly to the stock because they will not infuse in this way and will therefore not add flavour. They should be toasted slightly in a dry frying pan or skillet, or in the oven in a metal or enamelled baking pan, because saffron has a moisture content of 12 per cent and needs to be totally dry before use. Afterwards the saffron threads should be pounded in a mortar with a pestle (see photograph, page 21), mixed with a little hot stock and added to the rice halfway through the cooking time.

Personally, I prefer saffron to coloured powders because of its unique aroma. I use saffron from La Mancha. I prepare a certain amount of it in advance, diluting it in a little water, then I add it to recipes with a dropper when I need it. I keep this mixture in the refrigerator in an airtight container to prevent it from fermenting. You can also buy packets of saffron powder, but take care as there are many fake saffron powders on the market. If you buy ground saffron, it's best to choose the most reliable brand.

OTHER SPICES

Meeting Olivier Roellinger, the award-winning chef of the Maisons de Bricourt restaurant in Cancale, Brittany, in northwest France, changed my life. The way he uses spices differs from everything I thought I used to know about them. His influence revolutionized my cooking, and I would like to pay tribute to him here. Used wisely, spices can turn a dish into something truly special.

Taste is obviously fundamental to a cook's art. Each mouthful should be the most intense, the longest and richest possible, and the memory of it should be sublime. One single spoonful must be able to tell a complex story, and good cooking consists of making connections between foods. I aim to blend various spices in each recipe and to achieve harmony without compromising the basic principle. To flavour a stock, I first process the spices by toasting them lightly, before allowing them to infuse in the stock, which is left to stand covered in clingfilm (plastic wrap).

If you are cooking paella on a barbecue or outdoor grill, you can toast your spices in advance and put them into muslin (cheesecloth) packages or a spice bag made specifically for this purpose. Fabric tea bags, if you can find them, are also ideal. Add them to the paella at the same time as you add the stock, and remove them before the rice has absorbed much of the liquid, so that the flavour is distributed evenly (see photograph, page 29).

ÑORA PEPPERS

This round chilli pepper (see photograph, page 26), which is sold dried, is grown in Andalusia and less frequently in Morocco. It is known as a sweet pepper because of its mild and fruity taste. In the area around Alicante ñora peppers are a traditional accompaniment to paella. When you are buying ñora peppers make sure that they are not too dry and that they retain a hint of suppleness. Their taste is pleasant, intense, fruit-like and slightly bitter.

To use them, remove the stalks and seeds, tear the flesh into small pieces and sauté in olive oil with a little garlic. Next, put the mixture into a mortar and crush with the pestle, adding some coarse salt to aid the process. In Spain, poultry or game livers are sometimes added to the mix. This paste is then diluted with a little of the cooking liquid and added to the *sofrito*. Another method of using ñora peppers is to remove the stalk and seeds and soak them overnight in water. Drain them the following day, scrape the skin with a small, sharp knife to remove the flesh and add the flesh to your dish.

PIQUILLO PEPPERS

Another variety of sweet, aromatic, plump chilli pepper, piquillos are sold fresh, skinned and preserved in jars. They must be cooked before use to make them more digestible.

LEMON AND LIME

In Spain, lemon wedges are often served with paella. I use both lemons and limes as a flavouring, with the zest grated over the paella (see photograph, page 29) just before serving in order to add flavour to the dish without moistening or adding acidity to it. Subtlety is everything.

CHORIZO

Some cooks insist on adding cured Spanish chorizo sausage to paella. I feel that this is a mistake because the fat of the chorizo melts and seeps down to the bottom of the paella, and the sausage itself hardens when cooked. I think people use chorizo in paella because they like its taste of paprika, but if you add *pimentón* (sweet smoked paprika) to your paella, there is no need for chorizo!

COOKING PAELLA

A paella can be soft and moist, served with a *socarret* or crust, or it can have an extra-fine texture (see photograph, page 30). Extra-fine paella has the most interesting texture because the consistency of the rice changes in different parts of the pan. The variety of textures found within the same pan is what makes paella unique; it is also what makes the recipes in this book stand out from other rice-cooking techniques.

For the best flavour and texture, the easiest and most successful method is to start off the paella on the stove and carry out the rest of the cooking in the oven. If your oven is too small, however, you can cook the paella just on the stove. By oven I mean an ordinary electric oven, where the heat is constant. It is not necessary to have a fan-assisted oven. If you have a gas oven, you can adapt the way you use it according to the results obtained the first time you make paella.

When the paella rice is cooked, it should be allowed to rest for 2–4 minutes before serving. After this time it can no longer wait: you should eat immediately, otherwise the rice will continue to cook in the pan. If it is allowed to cool too much, the textures and flavours will change. They will not necessarily be unpleasant, but they will certainly be different. In Spain they like it hot – and fresh. Paella suffers greatly when re-heated. If a moist paella needs only another 2 minutes' cooking time, stir the rice with a fork and allow it to rest undisturbed. Distributing the heat in this way will complete the cooking.

COOKING PAELLA OUTSIDE

Historically, paella used to be cooked over a wood fire, often orange wood or vine prunings, lit either in the open air or in the fireplace. The ideal way to cook it is over wood, with the following proviso: this method does not enable you to achieve the 'extra-fine' texture. The smoke, on the other hand, imparts a delicious aroma to the paella. The ability to control the degree of heat precisely when cooking over wood or charcoal calls for great skill and forms part of the *paellero's* inherited know-how. The Sunday cook is expected to concentrate fully on the paella and to pay exceptional attention to detail.

Outdoor paella cooking can take place on a specially designed bar-becue or grill, or on an improvised one constructed with whatever materials are to hand – or the paella can even be cooked over a campfire. Specially designed barbecues for paella (also known as *paelleros*) are cylindrical brick constructions, with a circular grate, rather like a well, with a hood on top. They are equipped with a heat control system next to the trivet where you place the paella. The heat comes from below, never from above. The steam released during the simmering process ensures that all the rice is cooked. At the end of the cooking time all the liquid should have been absorbed and the rice should be tender. In order to achieve a fast boil at the beginning, you should start cooking over high heat. If the flames are not high enough, you can lower the trivet in order to bring the paella closer to the heat source. The paella pan can

opposite: Ñora peppers (see page 25)

also be shifted horizontally if a rudimentary barbecue is used. You should finish cooking the paella gently over the embers: with less liquid remaining you will need less heat. As it cooks, therefore, the paella goes from high heat to low. The heat of the embers is used to produce a good *socarret*, or crust.

Cooking over charcoal is easier to control and to master. It has the same aromatic advantages as cooking over wood, but it also has the same disadvantages when it comes to texture. A paella cooked over wood should have the position of the pan lowered from the flames to the embers as the cooking progresses and the liquid evaporates, but a paella cooked over charcoal should start off close to the charcoal and by the end of the cooking time it should be positioned higher, further away from the heat. At the *sofrito* stage, the paella needs heat that is even and not too intense. After this you can gradually move the position of the paella pan upwards, so that it is further away from the heat of the charcoal.

You can also use a portable gas burner. These come in a variety of sizes and are widely used in Spain; their key advantage is that the heat is easier to control. The larger models should only be used outdoors. In Spain, these *paelleros* are usually bought for country houses, where they replace or supplement barbecues and charcoal braziers, which are equally popular.

COOKING PAELLA IN THE KITCHEN

In your kitchen at home the most practical procedure is to begin cooking the paella on top of the stove, and once all the ingredients have been added and the rice begins to swell, to finish cooking it in the oven. The main advantage of cooking paella in the kitchen is that it enables you to adapt the heat to the diameter of the cooking vessel. You can buy detachable heat diffusers, about 20 cm (8 inches) in diameter, which can sit over a gas hob (burner). The second advantage comes with finishing the paella in the oven, which enables you to tweak the textures and to create an extra-fine paella. You can persevere, experiment, perfect your rice-cooking skills and delight your guests. If you have no oven, use a heavy-base paella pan, so that you can cook the paella entirely on the stove.

AT THE TABLE

TABLE SETTINGS AND UTENSILS

When full, a paella pan can be rather tricky to handle. While it is hot, protect your hands with a rolled-up dish towel or oven gloves (mitts) and lift it by the handles so that you do not burn yourself. To transfer it from the stove to the oven, grasp the handle with a towel, slide a large, long-handled metal fish slice (spatula) underneath the paella pan – in the centre halfway between the two handles – and lift the pan. This is the best method to avoid spilling or burning anything.

Grating lime zest (see page 25)

Frying the rice until translucent (see page 18)

Covering the pan with a cloth (see page 22)

Removing the bag of spices (see page 25)

Stirring the paella with a wooden spoon (page 31)

The *soccaret* (see page 18)

To set the pan on the table, at Fogón I use a metal trivet (*trevede*) similar to those used on traditional paella barbecues. In Spain, people set the paella pan on folded newspaper or on a glazed ceramic square that has a few breadcrumbs sprinkled on top of it to stabilize the pan. You can also set the pan on three large bolts arranged in a triangle on the table.

HOW TO EAT PAELLA

To appreciate the diversity of textures, you should eat paella straight from the pan because the differences in texture are destroyed when the rice is spooned onto plates. Each diner should be given a wooden spoon to help themselves. Cutlery is best avoided because metal has a distinctive taste and gives a metallic and cold sensation to the palate.

Paella has its own internal geography, and the size of each portion becomes obvious to those present when eating straight out of the pan. There are certain 'rules' to be observed. The paella will be split into two halves if there are two diners, into three triangles if there are three diners and so on. Each diner mentally maps out the boundaries of their portion, respecting the invisible lines dividing up the paella's surface. Everyone helps his or herself within this given area. The middle of the paella is treated as a communal space. If someone has to be served separately (such as a child or an invalid), their rice is taken from the middle of the dish. If a diner does not care for one ingredient, he or she moves it into the middle so that someone else may take it.

ACCOMPANIMENTS

A sauce or a salad is served with some paellas to add even more variety of taste or to give a sensation of freshness. Aioli (a purée of olive oil and garlic, page 36), for instance, is a traditional accompaniment for *a banda* paella rice and fish dishes, but I think it is a pity to drown the taste of the rice with too much garlic. All the subtlety of the dish is lost after the second spoonful.

In the Alicante area, seafood and fish paellas are served with Salmorreta (page 37), a cold sauce made of garlic, tomatoes, ñora peppers and parsley.

In my restaurant I serve no aioli or lemon wedges, but I can suggest alternatives. For example, if you turn to the recipe for the 'Alicante-Marseille Return' Paella Rice (page 113), the rice is prepared in the Alicante style and served with Piquillo Pepper Rouille (page 37). This is one of my most popular dishes.

I also serve salads with paella. They cleanse the palate without interfering with the overall feel of the dish. With Black Paella Rice with Cuttlefish Ink (page 74), I serve a salad of sliced green bell peppers; with sardine or vegetable paellas, a salad of finely sliced fennel. Over certain rice dishes, I sprinkle finely chopped tender spinach stalks. They add freshness and acidity, to the surprise and delight of my guests, and are quite a revelation for some. I also use very mild, young shallots, spring onions (scallions) and sometimes even Japanese garnishes based on seaweed and sesame seeds.

posite: Paella with extra-fine texture
ee page 27)

IT'S UP TO YOU TO EXPERIMENT!

It is impossible to define an 'authentic' paella recipe because paella is not a recipe, but rather a method of cooking linked to a particular utensil: the pan. Paella is a traditional dish and so by its very nature varies according to circumstances, periods in history and seasons. Paella typifies Spanish cuisine – it is as representative of the country as the national flag, and can evoke similar feelings. Nowadays, though, it is a culinary monument that warrants reinvention.

I have written this book for everyone who enjoys cooking and eating good food. I have not avoided techniques or procedures that may be familiar to professionals but less so for the home cook; instead I have explained them so that they are accessible to everyone. I have tried to make each recipe detailed enough so that everyone can make paellas that are both traditional and sophisticated.

I hope that these recipes provide you with inspiration and a grounding that enables you to create your own paellas at home, with your own ingredients, and wherever you live!

Alberto Herráiz

Opposite : Alberto Herráiz prepar
Asturian-style Sweet Paella Rice wi
Pineapple (page 18

BASIC RECIPES

SAUCES TO SERVE WITH PAELLA

The following sauces to accompany paellas should never be allowed to mask the natural flavour of the dish. Their role is primarily to provide variety, refreshing the palate and adding to our appreciation of the subtleties and highlights of the dishes. Salads based on raw vegetables also make excellent accompaniments. You can, for example, serve salads of spinach leaves, rocket (arugula), fennel or white cabbage with paella.

ALLOLI
AIOLI

Makes about 500 ml (2¼ cups)
Preparation time: 25 minutes

4 cloves garlic

500 ml (2¼ cups) olive or sunflower oil

salt and pepper

Aioli is the traditional accompaniment to some paellas, but I have to admit that I serve it very reluctantly. After two or three mouthfuls of paella mixed with aioli, the garlic has an increasingly powerful effect and the palate is no longer receptive to the subtleties of the dish. Nevertheless, the recipe is given here for those of you who would like to make it. If you are making a large quantity, you can prepare it in a blender or food processor.

Blanch the garlic cloves in a small pan of boiling water for 30 seconds. Repeat three times, changing the water each time and immersing the garlic in cold water after each blanching. Drain, halve each clove lengthwise and remove and discard the central shoots. Using a pestle pound the garlic in a mortar until a smooth paste forms. Gradually drizzle in the oil, adding it drop by drop at first until the mixture starts to come together and the desired consistency is reached. The aioli should be thick and smooth. Season with salt and pepper.

ALLOLI DE RÚCULA
ROCKET (ARUGULA) AIOLI

Makes about 800 ml (3½ cups)
Preparation time: 25 minutes

500 g (4 cups) rocket (arugula) leaves, washed and dried in a salad spinner

500 ml (2¼ cups) olive oil

3 cloves garlic, halved and central shoots removed

2 egg yolks

1 baked potato, skin removed

salt and pepper

You can make a variation of the basic aioli recipe above by adding rocket (arugula) and egg to make the finished aioli thicker, before emulsifying with the oil.

Blanch the rocket (arugula) for a few seconds in boiling salted water, drain in a colander, squeeze out any excess moisture and allow to cool. Transfer to a food processor and blend to a fine purée. With the motor running, gradually add the olive oil until smooth and well combined. Pass through a fine-mesh sieve and set aside. Blanch the garlic in a small pan of boiling water for 30 seconds. Repeat four times, changing the water each time and immersing the garlic in cold water after each blanching. Drain. Finely process the garlic in the rinsed-out bowl of the food processor. Add the egg yolks and cooked potato and blend until well mixed. With the motor running, very gradually drizzle in the rocket-flavoured oil – drop by drop at first, then in a thin, steady stream – until you have a smooth, homogenous sauce. Season with salt and pepper.

ROUILLE DE PIQUILLOS
PIQUILLO PEPPER ROUILLE

Makes about 600 ml (2½ cups)
Preparation: 10 minutes

2 cloves garlic, halved and central
shoots removed

1 baked potato, skin removed

70 g (2½ oz) piquillo peppers
preserved in oil, drained

1 large (US extra large) egg yolk

330 ml (scant 1½ cups) olive oil

salt and pepper

Specially created as an accompaniment to the 'Alicante–Marseille Return' Paella Rice (page 113), this is a variation on rouille *(the traditional accompaniment to bouillabaisse) as well as a tribute to it.*

Remove the central shoot of the garlic cloves and blanch them five times in boiling water, changing the water each time, and immersing them in cold water after each blanching. Drain. If you prefer a strong garlic flavour, blanch it fewer times. Using a hand-held electric blender, mix together the garlic, potato and piquillos until well blended. Add the egg yolk and process until combined. With the motor running, very gradually drizzle in the oil – drop by drop at first, then in a thin, steady stream – until the sauce is thick and smoothly emulsified. Season with salt and pepper.

SALMORRETA
SALMORRETA

Makes 300 ml (1¼ cups)
Preparation time: 15 minutes +
overnight soaking

dried ñora peppers, stalks removed
and seeded

ripe tomatoes

cloves garlic

sprigs of flat-leaf parsley

onion, very finely chopped

00 ml (scant 1 cup) olive oil

0 ml (scant ½ cup) red wine vinegar

erry vinegar, to taste

lt and pepper

In the Castellón region of Valencia, eastern Spain, you will often find this sauce served with seafood paellas.

The day before preparing the sauce, put the ñora peppers in a bowl of cold water, and let soak for at least 12 hours.

The next day, preheat the oven to 180°C/350°F/Gas Mark 4. Drain the ñora peppers. Using a small, sharp knife, scrape the flesh away from the skin. Discard the skin, and set the flesh aside. Roast the tomatoes in the oven until their skins have blackened slightly. Remove from the oven and, when cool enough to handle, skin and seed the tomatoes, and chop the flesh finely. Set aside.

Blanch the garlic in a small pan of boiling water for 30 seconds. Repeat twice, changing the water each time and immersing the garlic in cold water after each blanching. Drain. Halve each clove lengthwise, and remove and discard the central shoot.

Put the garlic, parsley and reserved flesh of the ñora peppers in a food processor. Season with salt and pepper, and blend to a purée. Add the onion and roasted tomato flesh. With the motor running, drizzle in the oil – drop by drop at first, then in a thin stream – and then the vinegar gradually until the sauce is smooth and emulsified.

STOCKS AND FUMETS

The stocks given on the following pages are specifically intended for paellas. They help to enhance the flavour of the other ingredients in the paella. The stock's flavour impregnates the rice and, because rice is the main ingredient of paella, the stock is a crucial stage of its preparation. Good-quality ready-made stocks can be substituted, but the results will be slightly different.

ADVICE FOR MAKING STOCKS AND FUMETS

Use a large, deep pan, stockpot or casserole. The pan should be nearly full – the liquid should come to within 3–6 cm (1¼–2½ inches) of the brim. Regularly remove any scum, fat or oil that rises to the surface with a skimmer or slotted spoon. The precise quantity you end up with will depend on the intensity of the heat the stock is cooked over.

Cover the pan with a tight-fitting lid during cooking and aim for a very gentle simmer with large bubbles. For fish and seafood stocks, simmer for 25 minutes; meat stocks need longer. Aromatic herbs and spices should be infused off the heat, in a covered pan.

For a clear stock or fumet, leave the layer of ingredients at the bottom of the pan undisturbed when you are straining the stock to prevent the liquid from becoming cloudy.

It's often easier to prepare a large quantity and reserve the rest for use in other recipes.

CALDO DE VERDURAS
VEGETABLE STOCK

Makes about 2.5 litres (10½ cups)
Preparation time: 15 minutes
Cooking time: 3 hours +
30 minutes for infusing

200 g (1½ cups) white turnips, finely diced

4 carrots, finely sliced into strips

2 celery stalks, finely sliced

2 leeks, well rinsed and finely sliced

1 fennel bulb, finely sliced

3 spring onions (scallions), finely sliced

1 shallot, finely sliced

2 tomatoes, diced

4 button (white) mushrooms, finely sliced

3 bay leaves

3 cloves garlic

3 sprigs of flat-leaf parsley

3 sprigs of dill

6 green cardamom pods

6 coriander seeds

1 clove

½ cinnamon stick

4 black peppercorns

6 dried juniper berries

This stock should be adapted according to your chosen paella recipe, but its ingredients will also depend on the season and what is available. The selection of vegetables given here is therefore only a suggestion. Avoid using vegetables that are prone to oxidizing and discoloration, such as artichokes, spinach or aubergines (eggplant). If you are short of time, a good-quality ready-made stock can be substituted, although the results will be different.

Put all the ingredients except the spices into a large, deep pan or stockpot, and pour over 3 litres (12½ cups) water. Bring to a boil, then reduce the heat to very low and simmer, covered, for 4 hours. Top up (top off) with more water if needed, and skim off any scum that rises to the surface every 30 minutes.

Almost at the end of the cooking time, toast the whole spices in a dry frying pan or skillet over medium heat for a few minutes until fragrant, shaking the pan occasionally so that they toast evenly; take care not to allow them to burn. Remove the pan of stock from the heat, and tip in the toasted spices. Cover and let infuse, off the heat, for 30 minutes. Carefully strain the stock through a fine-mesh sieve or chinois, leaving behind the ingredients that have settled on the bottom of the pan to prevent the stock from becoming cloudy; discard the solids. Allow the stock to cool, then chill in the refrigerator, covered, until needed.

CALDO DE BULLABESA
BOUILLABAISSE STOCK

Makes about 2.5 litres (10½ cups)
Preparation time: 25 minutes +
6 hours' marinating
Cooking time: 20 minutes

1 fennel bulb

1 onion

1 leek, white part only

6 cloves garlic, finely chopped

2 bay leaves

4 sprigs of thyme

10 sprigs of flat-leaf parsley

zest of 1 unwaxed orange

200 ml (scant 1 cup) olive oil

2 kg (4½ lb) small rock fish such as
mullet, gurnard (sea robin) or scorpion
fish, cleaned, scaled and gills removed

200 g (7 oz) very ripe tomatoes

4 whole small shore (green) crabs

60 ml (¼ cup) pastis liqueur

Cut the fennel, onion and leek into 1-cm (½-inch) dice and place in a non-reactive shallow dish or bowl. Add the garlic, bay leaves, thyme, flat-leaf parsley, orange zest and olive oil. Stir through. Use to marinate the fish, covered, in the refrigerator for 6 hours. Cut the tomato into quarters and clean the crabs.

Tip the fish and its marinade into a large, deep pan or stockpot, then add the crabs. Once the ingredients have started to brown lightly, add the tomatoes and sauté over medium heat until the tomatoes have broken up and started to disintegrate.

Pour in 3 litres (12½ cups) water and bring to a boil. Reduce the heat to as low as possible, cover and simmer very gently for 20 minutes, then add the pastis. Using a ladle, strain the stock first through a medium-mesh sieve, then a second time through a fine-mesh sieve or chinois; discard the solids. Allow the stock to cool, then chill in the refrigerator until needed.

CALDO DE BACALAO
SALT COD STOCK

Makes about 3 litres (12½ cups)
Preparation time: 25 minutes
Cooking time: 60 minutes +
15 minutes for infusing

100 ml (scant ½ cup) olive oil

1 leek, finely sliced

1 carrot, finely sliced into strips

1 small celery stalk, finely sliced

1 onion, finely chopped

1 fennel bulb, finely sliced

1 dried ñora pepper, stalk removed
and seeded, coarsely crumbled

2 bay leaves

2 cloves garlic, halved

100 ml (scant ½ cup) dry white wine

3 kg (6¾ lb) salt cod skin and
bones, soaked in several changes
of cold water

2 sage leaves

Heat the olive oil in a large, deep pan or stockpot, and sauté the leek, carrot, celery, onion and fennel over low heat for 5 minutes until softened and starting to colour. Add the ñora pepper, bay leaves and garlic. Cook until lightly browned. Pour in the white wine and deglaze the pan, scraping up any bits on the bottom with a wooden spoon or spatula. Cook until all the vegetables have softened and the alcohol has evaporated.

Pour in sufficient cold water to fill the pan. Add the salt cod skin and bones. Increase the heat and bring to a simmer, skimming frequently; do not allow to boil. Cover, reduce the heat and simmer very gently for 60 minutes, skimming off any scum that rises to the surface at frequent intervals.

At the end of the cooking time, remove the pan from the heat. Remove any remaining oil by lowering a sheet of paper towel briefly onto the surface of the stock. Add the sage, cover and let infuse, off the heat, for 15 minutes. Carefully strain the fumet through a fine-mesh sieve or chinois, leaving behind the ingredients that have settled on the bottom of the pan to prevent the fumet from becoming cloudy; discard the solids. Allow to cool, then chill in the refrigerator until needed.

CALDO DE ANGUILA
EEL STOCK

Makes about 2.5 litres (10½ cups)
Preparation time: 15 minutes
Cooking time: 20 minutes +
30 minutes for infusing

100 ml (scant ½ cup) sesame oil

head and bones of 1 eel, gills and eyes removed, chopped into pieces

1 leek, finely sliced

1 carrot, finely sliced into strips

1 small celery stalk, finely sliced

1 onion, finely chopped

1 fennel bulb, finely sliced

2 tomatoes, diced

3 bay leaves

3 cloves garlic, finely chopped

1 dried ñora pepper, stalk removed and seeded, coarsely crumbled

100 ml (scant ½ cup) mirin

100 ml (scant ½ cup) Japanese eel sauce (unagi kabayaki no tare)

3 tablespoons coriander seeds

2 lemongrass stalks

finely grated zest of 1 lime

1½ tablespoons freshly grated ginger

Put the sesame oil in a large, deep pan or stockpot and brown the eel head and bones for a few minutes. Add the vegetables, tomatoes, bay leaves, garlic and ñora pepper. Sauté until the vegetables are softened and starting to colour. Add the mirin and Japanese eel sauce, and pour in 2 litres (8½ cups) cold water. Bring to a boil, then reduce the heat to low. Simmer very gently, covered, for 25 minutes, skimming off any scum that rises to the surface.

Almost at the end of the cooking time, toast the coriander seeds in a dry frying pan or skillet over medium heat for a few minutes until fragrant, shaking the pan occasionally so that they toast evenly; take care not to burn them. In a small bowl, mix together the toasted coriander seeds, lemongrass, lime zest and ginger.

Remove the pan of stock from the heat, and add the bowl of flavourings. Cover and let infuse, off the heat, for 40 minutes. Skim off any oil with a ladle, using a sheet of paper towel lightly dropped on the surface of the stock for a few seconds to absorb any remaining oil. Carefully strain the stock through a fine-mesh sieve or chinois. The stock should be very clear. Allow to cool, then chill in the refrigerator.

CALDO DE BONITO
BONITO STOCK

Makes about 3 litres (12½ cups)
Preparation time: 40 minutes
Cooking time: 25 minutes + 20 minutes for infusing

3 kg (6 lb 12 oz) bonito heads and bones, gills removed and rinsed

100 ml (scant ½ cup) olive oil

1 leek, finely sliced

1 celery stalk, finely sliced

1 carrot, finely sliced into strips

1 fennel bulb, finely sliced

1 onion, finely sliced

3 cloves garlic, finely sliced

2 tomatoes, diced

3 bay leaves

1 dried ñora pepper, stalk removed and seeded, coarsely crumbled

100 ml (scant ½ cup) dry white wine

2×40-g (1½-oz) packets dried bonito flakes (katsuobushi)

Preheat the oven to 150°C/300°F/Gas Mark 2. Put the rinsed bonito heads and bones in a roasting pan, sprinkle with half the olive oil and roast in the oven for about 30 minutes until lightly browned.

Meanwhile, heat the remaining oil in a large pan or stockpot over low heat. Add the vegetables, garlic, tomatoes, bay leaves and ñora pepper, and gently sauté until softened and starting to colour. Pour in the white wine and deglaze the pan, scraping up any bits on the bottom with a wooden spoon or spatula. Once the alcohol has evaporated, add the roasted fish heads and bones. Pour in 3 litres (12½ cups) cold water, and bring to a boil. Reduce the heat, cover and simmer very gently for 25 minutes, frequently skimming off any scum that rises to the surface.

Remove the pan from the heat, add the dried bonito flakes, cover and let infuse, off the heat, for 20 minutes. Carefully strain the stock through a fine-mesh sieve or chinois. The stock should be very clear. Allow to cool, then chill in the refrigerator.

FONDO DE SEPIA
CUTTLEFISH STOCK

Makes about 800 ml (3½ cups)
Preparation time: 30 minutes +
at least 12 hours' soaking
Cooking time: 30 minutes

2 dried ñora peppers, stalks removed and seeded

200 ml (scant 1 cup) olive oil

1 leek, cut into 1-cm (½-inch) dice

1 celery stalk, cut into 1-cm (½-inch) dice

2 carrots, cut into 1-cm (½-inch) dice

2 red onions, cut into 1-cm (½-inch) dice

1 garlic bulb, halved crosswise

1 sprig of rosemary

2 sprigs of lemon thyme

2 bay leaves

500 g (1 lb 2 oz) cuttlefish heads and trimmings, rinsed and finely chopped

100 ml (scant ½ cup) white wine

8 ripe tomatoes, cut into quarters

500 ml (2 cups) Fish Fumet (page 48)

pinch of sugar

pinch of ground ginger

salt and pepper

The day before preparing the stock, put the ñora peppers in a bowl of cold water and let soak overnight. The following day, drain the peppers and scrape the flesh away from the skins with a small, sharp knife. Discard the skin and set aside the flesh.

Heat the olive oil in a large, deep pan or stockpot, and gently sauté the leek, celery, carrots, onions and garlic bulb over low heat for about 10 minutes until the vegetables are softened and translucent. Add the rosemary, lemon thyme and bay leaves, and stir through well.

Add the cuttlefish heads and trimmings, and stir thoroughly. Continue cooking over low heat until all the ingredients have cooked and softened, then add the reserved ñora peppers. Pour in the white wine, and deglaze the pan, scraping up any bits on the bottom with a wooden spoon or spatula. Once the alcohol has evaporated, add the tomatoes and pour in the Fish Fumet. Bring to a boil, then reduce the heat and simmer very gently over low heat for 30 minutes, stirring well every 5 minutes, until the tomatoes are cooked and broken down.

Transfer the contents of the pan to a blender or food processor, blend to a purée and season with salt and pepper. Add the sugar – to counteract the acidity of the tomato – then the ginger.

Carefully strain the stock through a fine-mesh sieve or chinois into a clean pan (discard the solids), and reduce over medium heat for 10–15 minutes until very thick. Stir frequently to prevent the stock from catching and burning on the bottom of the pan.Remove from the heat and allow to cool completely. Transfer to an airtight container, and chill in the refrigerator.

FONDO PARA FIDEUÁ DE MARISCOS
SEAFOOD STOCK FOR FIDEUÁ

Makes about 500 ml (2¼ cups)
Preparation time: 15 minutes
Cooking time: 25 minutes +
30 minutes for infusing

100 ml (scant ½ cup) olive oil

1 leek, finely sliced

1 onion, finely chopped

2 small celery stalks, finely sliced

2 carrots, finely sliced into strips

6 cloves garlic, finely chopped

3 tomatoes, diced

2 bay leaves

1 sprig of rosemary

3 sprigs of flat-leaf parsley

1 kg (2¼ lb) rock fish such as mullet, gurnard (sea robin) or scorpion fish, cleaned, scaled and gills removed, chopped into pieces

2 whole shore (green) crabs or 3 whole small green or other swimming crabs (such as blue crab), cleaned, rinsed and cut in two

50 ml (¼ cup) pastis liqueur

1 lemongrass stalk, bruised and finely sliced

Spices and flavourings

1 teaspoon freeze-dried green peppercorns

1 teaspoon coriander seeds

20 g (¾ oz) dried fennel stalks

¼ teaspoon freshly grated ginger

1 dried ñora pepper, stalk removed and seeded, coarsely crumbled

Heat the olive oil in a large, deep pan or stockpot over low heat, and add the leek, onion, celery, carrots, garlic, tomatoes, bay leaves, rosemary and parsley. Sauté very gently for about 20 minutes until the vegetables have softened and any liquid reduced.

Add the fish pieces and crabs, and continue to cook until lightly browned. Add the pastis and lemongrass and deglaze the the pan, scraping up any bits on the bottom with a wooden spoon or spatula. Once the alcohol has evaporated, cover the contents of the pan completely with water. Bring to a boil, skim off any scum that rises to the surface, then reduce the heat. Barely simmer over low heat for 5 minutes, skimming frequently. Top up (top off) with more water as needed to compensate for evaporation.

Meanwhile, toast the green peppercorns and coriander seeds in a dry frying pan or skillet over medium heat for a couple of minutes until fragrant; take care not to burn. Add to the other spices and flavourings.

Carefully strain the stock into a clean heavy pan; discard the solids. Bring to a boil, and continue boiling until the stock has reduced to 500 ml (2¼ cups). Remove from the heat. Add the spices and flavourings to the pan, cover and let infuse, off the heat, for 30 minutes. Carefully strain the stock once more through a fine-mesh sieve or chinois, leaving behind the ingredients that have settled on the bottom of the pan to prevent the stock from becoming cloudy. Allow to cool, then chill in the refrigerator.

BASIC RECIPE

FONDO DE GAMBAS Y SALMONETE
PRAWN (SHRIMP) AND RED MULLET STOCK

Makes about 800 ml (3½ cups)
Preparation time: 25 minutes +
at least 12 hours' soaking
Cooking time: 30 minutes

2 dried ñora peppers

100 ml (scant ½ cup) olive oil

1 leek, cut into 1-cm (½-inch) dice

1 celery stalk, cut into 1-cm (½-inch)
dice

1 onion, cut into 1-cm (½-inch) dice

2 carrots, cut into 1-cm (½-inch) dice

1 garlic bulb, halved crosswise

200 g (7 oz) uncooked king prawn
(jumbo shrimp) heads, peeled

1 sprig of rosemary

2 sprigs of lemon thyme

2 bay leaves

red mullet livers (use the livers
reserved from making the paella)

50 ml (¼ cup) brandy

4 tomatoes, cut into quarters

500 ml (2¼ cups) red mullet fumet
(follow the recipe for Rock fish Fumet
on page 49, using only red mullet)

pinch of sugar

pinch of ground ginger

salt and pepper

The day before preparing the stock, soak the ñora peppers in a bowl of cold water. The following day, drain the peppers and scrape the flesh away from the skins with a small, sharp knife. Discard the skin and set aside the flesh.

Heat the olive oil in a large, deep pan or stockpot over low heat, and gently sauté the vegetables, garlic and prawn (shrimp) heads for about 5 minutes until the vegetables have softened. Add the rosemary, lemon thyme and bay leaves, and stir together thoroughly. Add the mullet livers and continue cooking over low heat until the mixture has reduced and thickened. Tip in the reserved ñora peppers and stir through.

Pour in the brandy and deglaze the pan, scraping up any bits on the bottom with a wooden spoon or spatula. Once the alcohol has evaporated, add the tomatoes and pour in the red mullet fumet. Bring to a boil, then reduce the heat and simmer very gently indeed over low heat for 30 minutes, stirring every 5 minutes, until the tomatoes are cooked and broken down.

Transfer the contents of the pan to a blender or food processor, and blend to a purée. Season with salt and pepper. Add the sugar – to counteract the acidity of the tomato – then the ginger.

Carefully strain the stock through a fine-mesh sieve or chinois into a clean pan, pressing the ingredients down into the sieve with a wooden spoon or spatula; discard the solids. Reduce the stock over medium heat for 10–15 minutes. Stir frequently to prevent it from catching and burning on the bottom of the pan.

Remove from the heat and allow to cool completely. Transfer to an airtight container and chill in the refrigerator until needed.

FONDO NEGRO
BLACK STOCK

Makes about 800 ml (3½ cups)
Preparation time: 25 minutes +
overnight soaking
Cooking time: 30 minutes

2 dried ñora peppers, stalks removed
and seeded

500 g (1 lb 2 oz) small shore (green)
crabs, clean, rinsed and halved

200 ml (scant 1 cup) olive oil

1 leek, cut into 1-cm (½-inch) dice

1 celery stalk, cut into 1-cm (½-inch)
dice

2 red onions, cut into 1-cm (½-inch)
dice

2 carrots, cut into 1-cm (½-inch) dice

1 garlic bulb, halved crosswise

1 kg (2¼ lb) tomatoes, cut into quarters

1 sprig of rosemary

2 sprigs of lemon thyme

2 bay leaves

50 ml (¼ cup) pastis liqueur

1 litre (4¼ cups) Fish Fumet (page 48)

pinch of sugar

pinch of ground ginger

10 g (¼ oz) cuttlefish or squid ink
(available from good fish suppliers)

salt and pepper

There are differences of opinion when it comes to black rice. Some people prefer to call it 'grey rice' because this is often its true colour. I prefer my 'black' rice to be as dark as possible. Nowadays you can use untreated frozen cuttlefish ink. This is a high-quality product that enables you to obtain your preferred colour, either towards grey or towards black. In days gone by the depth of colour depended on the size of the cuttlefish used in the recipe. I prefer to use the more tender small cuttlefish, and to use not only their natural ink, but also some of the concentrated variety, bought separately. If you are short of time, you could substitute good-quality ready-made fish stock to which 10 g (¼ oz) cuttlefish or squid ink has been added, although the result will of course be different.

The day before preparing the stock, put the ñora peppers in a bowl of cold water and let soak overnight. The following day, drain the peppers and scrape the flesh away from the skins with a knife. Discard the skin and reserve the flesh.

Preheat the oven to 150°C/300°F/Gas Mark 2. Roast the crabs in the oven for 10 minutes. Set aside.

Heat the olive oil in a large, deep pan or stockpot over low heat. Add the leek, celery, onions, carrots and garlic, and gently sauté for about 10 minutes until soft and translucent. Add the rosemary, lemon thyme and bay leaf, and stir well for another couple of minutes until the herbs have softened.

Add the reserved ñora peppers. Pour in the pastis and deglaze the pan, scraping up any bits on the bottom with a wooden spatula. Stir in the roasted crabs, then add the tomatoes. Set aside a little of the Fish Fumet to dilute the cuttlefish ink, then pour the remainder into the pan. Bring to a boil, then reduce the heat to low once again. Simmer very gently indeed for 30 minutes, stirring every 5 minutes, until the tomatoes are cooked and broken down.

Allow to cool a little, then transfer the contents of the pan to a food processor or blender. Blend until smooth. Season with salt and pepper. Add the sugar – to counteract the acidity of the tomatoes – then the ginger. Blend again briefly.

Carefully strain the stock through a fine-mesh sieve or chinois into a clean pan, to get rid of any crab shell fragments. Dilute the cuttlefish ink with the reserved Fish Fumet, and stir into the fumet in the pan. Reduce over medium heat for 10–15 minutes. Stir frequently to prevent the stock from catching and burning on the bottom of the pan.

Remove from the heat and allow to cool completely. Transfer to an airtight container and chill in the refrigerator until needed.

LANGOUSTINE AND MUSHROOM FUMET

Makes 2.5 litres (10½ cups)
Preparation time: 15 minutes
Cooking time: 20 minutes +
30 minutes for infusing

trimmings from the mushrooms used
in the paella recipe

heads and claws of 4 langoustines
(use the heads and claws reserved
from the paella recipe)

100 ml (scant ½ cup) olive oil

1 leek, cut into fine strips

1 onion, finely chopped

2 celery stalks, cut into fine strips

1 tomato, finely chopped

100 g (1 cup) fennel bulb, cut into
fine strips

200 ml (scant 1 cup) white wine

1 bouquet garni (bay leaf, garlic,
rosemary, thyme, lemon zest)

Spices and flavourings

15 g (3 tablespoons) coriander seeds

15 freeze-dried green peppercorns

1 lime

1 lemongrass stalk, bruised
and chopped

1½ teaspoons freshly grated ginger

This fumet can be made with the trimmings from the mushrooms used in the Paella Rice with Langoustines and Cep (Porcini) Mushrooms on page 112.

Rinse and drain the mushrooms or mushroom trimmings, making sure that there is no earth or grit left on them. Pat dry thoroughly with paper towels. Crush the langoustines' claws (a nutcracker works well).

Heat the oil in a large, deep pan or stockpot over medium heat, and add the langoustine heads and claws. Sauté until starting to brown, then add the mushroom trimmings. Continue sautéing gently for a few moments, then add the leek, onion, celery, tomato and fennel. Cook over medium heat for 2 minutes.

Pour in the white wine and deglaze the pan, scraping up any bits on the bottom with a wooden spatula. Allow the wine to reduce a little. Once the alcohol has evaporated, pour in 2.5 litres (10½ cups) water, and add the bouquet garni. Bring to a boil, skim off any scum that rises to the surface, then reduce the heat to low. Simmer very gently, covered, for 20 minutes, skimming frequently.

Meanwhile, toast the coriander seeds and green peppercorns in a dry frying pan or skillet until fragrant. Finely grate the zest of the lime, avoiding any white pith. After 20 minutes, remove the pan from the heat. Stir in the toasted spices, lime zest, lemongrass and ginger. Cover and let infuse, off the heat, for 30 minutes.

Strain the fumet slowly through a fine-mesh sieve or chinois, tipping the pan carefully on an angle. Allow to cool completely. Transfer to an airtight container and chill in the refrigerator.

FUMÉ DE MARISCO
SHELLFISH FUMET

Makes about 3 litres (12½ cups)
Preparation time: 25 minutes
Cooking time: 25 minutes +
40 minutes for infusing

100 ml (scant ½ cup) olive oil

1 leek, cut into fine strips

1 carrot, cut into fine strips

1 small celery stalk, cut into fine strips

1 onion, finely chopped

2 tomatoes, diced

3 cloves garlic

3 sprigs of flat-leaf parsley

3 bay leaves

1 kg (2¼ lb) uncooked shellfish heads
(such as small shrimp, king prawns
(jumbo shrimp), langoustine or mantis
shrimps), rinsed

300 g (11 oz) small shore (green)
crabs, cleaned and rinsed

1 dried ñora pepper, stalk removed and
seeded, coarsely crumbled

200 ml (scant 1 cup) dry white wine

Spices and flavourings

½ teaspoon freeze-dried green
peppercorns

½ teaspoon coriander seeds

50 g (½ cup) fresh ginger, finely sliced

2 sprigs of lemon thyme

2 lemongrass stalks, bruised and finely
chopped

zest of 2 limes, finely grated

If you are short of time, a good-quality ready-made fish stock can be substituted, in which you can infuse the heads and shells of the shellfish for 25 minutes. The results will, however, be slightly different.

Heat the oil in a large, deep pan or stockpot and add the leek, carrot, celery, onion and tomato. Gently sauté until starting to soften and turn translucent, then add the garlic, parsley and bay leaves. Continue cooking over low heat until just starting to colour; do not allow to burn. Add the shellfish heads, crabs and ñora peppers, and sauté until lightly browned all over.

Pour in the white wine, and deglaze the pan, scraping up any bits on the bottom with a wooden spatula. Once the alcohol has evaporated, fill the pan with cold water. Bring to a boil, skim off any scum that rises to the surface, then reduce the heat to low and simmer very gently for 25 minutes, skimming frequently.

Meanwhile, toast the green peppercorns and coriander seeds in a dry frying pan or skillet until fragrant. After 25 minutes, remove the pan from the heat. Stir the toasted spices, ginger, lemon thyme, lemongrass and lime zest into the fumet, cover and let infuse, off the heat, for 40 minutes. Using a ladle, skim off any oil that has risen to the top; remove any remaining oil by lowering a sheet of paper towel briefly onto the surface. Carefully strain the fumet through a fine-mesh sieve or chinois, leaving behind the ingredients that have settled on the bottom of the pan to prevent the stock from becoming cloudy. Allow to cool completely. Transfer to an airtight container and chill in the refrigerator.

FUMÉ DE PESCADO
FISH FUMET

Makes about 3 litres (12½ cups)
Preparation time: 50 minutes
Cooking time: 25 minutes +
40 minutes for infusing

3 kg (6½ lb) white fish bones and heads
(such as turbot, red mullet, monkfish,
cod or hake, sole) and gills removed

100 ml (scant ½ cup) olive oil

1 leek, cut into fine strips

1 carrot, cut into fine strips

1 small celery stalk, cut into fine strips

1 fennel bulb, cut into fine strips

1 onion, finely chopped

2 tomatoes, diced

3 cloves garlic, finely chopped

3 bay leaves

1 dried ñora pepper, stalk removed and
seeded, coarsely crumbled

100 ml (scant ½ cup) dry white wine

Spices and flavourings

1 teaspoon green anise seeds

1 teaspoon freeze-dried green
peppercorns

1 star anise

2 dried fennel stalks

2 sprigs of flat-leaf parsley

1 teaspoon black peppercorns

If you are short of time, good-quality ready-made fish stock can be substituted, although the result will be different.

Preheat the oven to 150°C/300°F/Gas Mark 2. Thoroughly rinse the fish bones and heads, and arrange in a layer in a roasting pan. Sprinkle with half the olive oil, and roast in the oven for 30 minutes until lightly browned.

Towards the end of the roasting time, heat the remaining oil in a large, deep pan or stockpot and add the leek, carrot, celery, fennel, onion and tomatoes. Gently sauté until starting to soften and turn translucent, then add the garlic, bay leaves and ñora pepper. Continue cooking over low heat until lightly browned; do not allow to burn.

Pour in the white wine and deglaze the pan, scraping up any bits on the bottom with a wooden spatula. Once the alcohol has evaporated, add the browned fish heads and bones to the pan and fill the pan with cold water. Bring to a boil, then skim off any scum that has risen to the surface. Reduce the heat to low and simmer very gently, covered, for 25 minutes, skimming frequently.

Meanwhile, toast the anise seeds and green peppercorns in a dry frying pan or skillet until fragrant. Remove the pan from the heat. Add to the other spices and flavourings in a small bowl.

After 25 minutes, remove the pan from the heat. Stir in the spices and flavourings. Cover and let infuse off the heat for 40 minutes. Using a ladle, skim off any oil that has risen to the top; remove any remaining oil by lowering a sheet of paper towel briefly onto the surface. Carefully strain the fumet through a fine-mesh sieve or chinois, without disturbing the ingredients that have settled on the bottom of the pan. Allow to cool completely and chill in the refrigerator until needed.

FUMÉ DE PESCADO DE ROCA
ROCK FISH FUMET

Makes about 3 litres (12½ cups)
Preparation time: 55 minutes
Cooking time: 25 minutes +
30 minutes for infusing

2 kg (4½ lb) rock fish such as red mullet, gurnard (sea robin) or scorpion fish, cleaned, scaled and gills removed

100 ml (scant ½ cup) olive oil

1 leek, cut into fine strips

1 carrot, cut into fine strips

1 celery stalk, cut into fine strips

1 onion, finely sliced

1 fresh fennel bulb, finely sliced

2 tomatoes, diced

300 g (11 oz) small shore (green) crabs, rinsed

3 cloves garlic, finely chopped

3 bay leaves

1 dried ñora pepper, stalk removed, coarsely crumbled

100 ml (scant ½ cup) dry white wine or pastis liqueur

spices and flavourings

1 teaspoon green anise seeds

1 teaspoon green peppercorns

1 teaspoon black peppercorns

1 star anise

dried fennel stalks

sprigs of flat-leaf parsley

1 stalk liquorice

If you are short of time, a good-quality ready-made fish stock can be substituted, although the results will be different.

Preheat the oven to 150°C/300°F/Gas Mark 2. Arrange the fish in a layer in a roasting pan, sprinkle with half the olive oil and roast in the oven for 30 minutes until lightly browned.

Towards the end of the roasting time, heat the remaining oil in a large, deep pan or stockpot over low heat. Add the leek, carrot, celery, onion, fennel and tomatoes. Gently sauté until starting to soften and turn translucent, then add the crabs. Sauté for a few minutes, then add the garlic, bay leaves and ñora pepper. Continue cooking over low heat until lightly browned; do not allow to burn.

Pour in the white wine or pastis and deglaze the pan, scraping up any bits on the bottom with a wooden spatula. Once the alcohol has evaporated, add the roasted fish to the pan and fill the pan with cold water. Bring to a boil, then skim off any scum that has risen to the surface. Reduce the heat to low and simmer very gently, covered, for 25 minutes, skimming frequently.

Remove the pan from the heat. Stir in the spices and flavourings. Cover and let infuse, off the heat, for 30 minutes. Carefully strain the fumet through a fine-mesh sieve or chinois, leaving behind the ingredients that have settled on the bottom of the pan to prevent it from becoming cloudy. Allow to cool completely and chill in the refrigerator until needed.

CALDO DE CERDO
PORK STOCK

Makes about 4 litres (16 cups)
Preparation time: 25 minutes
Cooking time: 3 hours + 30 minutes
for infusing

50 ml (¼ cup) olive oil

2 kg (4½ lb) pork loin, cut into small pieces

1 pig's foot, cut into thick sections

400 g (14 oz) pork spare ribs, cut into small pieces

100 g (3½ oz) Ibérico ham, or any other cured ham, in one piece

½ leek, cut into fine strips

1 celery stalk, cut into fine strips

1 onion, finely chopped

1 carrot, cut into fine strips

100 g (¾ oz) turnips (use long or round varieties), cut into fine strips

100 ml (scant ½ cup) dry white wine

herbs and spices as listed under relevant paella recipes

Put the olive oil in a large, deep pan or stockpot, and brown all the meat; remove the meat from the pan when lightly browned, and let drain in a large sieve or colander set over a bowl or dish. Return the drained meat to the pan and add the vegetables. Cook, stirring continuously, for 5 minutes until the vegetables have softened. Pour in the white wine and deglaze the pan, scraping up any bits on the bottom with a wooden spatula. Let bubble for a minute or two until the wine has evaporated.

Pour in 4 litres (16 cups) water. Bring to a boil over very high heat, then skim off any fat or scum. Reduce the heat to low and simmer, covered, for 3 hours, skimming regularly.

Remove the pan from the heat, add the appropriate spices and herbs, stir and cover again. Let infuse, off the heat, for 30 minutes. Carefully strain the stock through a fine-mesh sieve or chinois. The stock should be very clear. Allow to cool completely, transfer to an airtight container and chill in the refrigerator.

CALDO DE JAMÓN IBÉRICO
IBÉRICO HAM STOCK

Makes about 2.5 litres (10½ cups)
Preparation time: 25 minutes
Cooking time: 3 hours + 30 minutes
for infusing

50 ml (¼ cup) olive oil

½ leek, cut into fine strips

1 celery stalk, cut into fine strips

1 onion, finely chopped

1 carrot, cut into fine strips

100 g (3½ oz) turnips (use long or round varieties)

50 g (scant ½ cup) hazelnuts

100 g (3½ oz) Ibérico ham rind and unsaturated fat

1 Ibérico ham bone, cut into 6 sections

1 tablespoon coriander seeds

1 tablespoon green cardamom pods

2 tablespoons black peppercorns

2 cloves

2 sprigs of rosemary

2 sprigs of thyme

Use the pink layer of ham fat, not the oxidized, light-brown layer.

Pour the olive oil into a large, deep pan or stockpot over low heat. Gently sauté the leek, celery, onion, carrot, turnips and hazelnuts for 5 minutes. Add the ham rind and fat, and cook over fairly low heat. Add the ham bone and continue cooking until all the ingredients are lightly browned. Pour in 3 litres (12½ cups) water. Bring to a boil over very high heat, then skim any fat or scum that has risen the surface. Reduce the heat to low and simmer, covered, for 3 hours, skimming several times.

Meanwhile, toast the coriander, cardamom and black peppercorns in a dry frying pan or skillet until fragrant. Add to the other spices and flavourings in a small bowl.

At the end of the 3 hours' cooking time, remove the pan from the heat. Tip in the spices and flavourings, and stir through. Cover and let infuse, off the heat, for 30 minutes. Carefully strain the stock through a fine-mesh sieve or chinois. The stock should be very clear. Allow to cool completely and chill in the refrigerator.

CALDO DE CODORNIZ
QUAIL STOCK

Preparation time: 25 minutes
Cooking time: 3 hours
Makes about 2.5 litres (10½ cups)

8 oven-ready quail, coarsely chopped

150 g (5 oz) lardons or finely chopped bacon

50 ml (¼ cup) olive oil

1 leek, cut into fine strips

1 carrot, cut into fine strips

1 celery stalk, cut into fine strips

1 onion, finely chopped

1 tomato, diced

3 cloves garlic, finely chopped

2 bay leaves

3 sprigs of flat-leaf parsley

100 ml (scant ½ cup) red wine

Preheat the oven to 150°C/300°F/Gas Mark 2. Roast the quail and lardons in the oven for 15 minutes. Place in a metal sieve placed over a bowl so that the fat can drain off.

Meanwhile, heat the oil in a large pan or stockpot over low heat. Add the vegetables, garlic, bay leaves and parsley, and gently sauté for 5 minutes until lightly browned. Add the tomato, roast quail and lardons, and stir through. Pour in the red wine and deglaze the pan, scraping up any bits on the bottom of the pan with a wooden spatula. Once the alcohol has evaporated, pour in 3 litres (12½ cups) water. Bring to a boil, then skim off any scum. Reduce the heat to low and simmer very gently, covered, for 6 hours, skimming several times.

Remove the pan from the heat. Carefully strain the stock through a fine-mesh sieve or chinois; discard the solids. The stock should be very clear. Allow to cool completely and chill in the refrigerator.

CALDO DE POLLO O DE CONEJO
CHICKEN OR RABBIT STOCK

Makes 3–4 litres (12½–16 cups)
Preparation time: 25 minutes
Cooking time: 3 hours + 30 minutes for infusing

uncooked chicken carcass or the bones from a boned uncooked rabbit, cut into pieces

tablespoons sunflower oil

leek, cut into small dice

carrot, cut into small dice

celery stalk, cut into small dice

tomatoes, cut into small dice

onion, cut into small dice

cloves garlic

10 ml (scant ½ cup) white wine

bay leaves

sprigs of flat-leaf parsley

herbs and spices as listed under the relevant paella recipes

You can use chicken or rabbit for this stock, or both. If you are short of time, good-quality ready-made stock can be substituted, although the result will be different.

Preheat the oven to 150°C/300°F/Gas Mark 2. Put the chicken carcass or rabbit bones in a roasting pan. Sprinkle with half the olive oil and roast for 15 minutes until lightly browned. Pour the remaining oil into a large pan or stockpot over low heat. Add the vegetables and garlic and sauté until softened. Add the roasted carcasses, reserving the cooking juices and oil in the roasting pan. Stir, add the white wine and let the alcohol evaporate, then fill the pan with cold water. Bring to a boil, skimming off any scum regularly. Add the bay leaf and flat-leaf parsley.

Pour off the oil from the roasting pan into a separate pan. Deglaze the roasting pan with a little of the stock, scraping up any bits on the bottom with a wooden spatula. Add this liquid to the pan containing the stock, cover and simmer over low heat for 2½ hours, skimming from time to time.

Remove the pan from the heat, add the appropriate spices and herbs, and stir through. Cover and let infuse, off the heat, for 30 minutes. Carefully strain the stock through a fine-mesh sieve or chinois, leaving behind the ingredients that have settled on the bottom of the pan to prevent the stock from becoming cloudy. Allow to cool completely and chill in the refrigerator.

BASIC PREPARATIONS AND SOFRITOS

A technique as much as a combination of ingredients, *sofrito* forms the base for stocks and fumets, as well as other dishes, and consists of ingredients that are gently sautéed in olive oil. It is used throughout the Mediterranean as a basic preparation (known as *mirepoix* in France, *soffrito* in Italy and *refugado* in Portugal) and most notably in Spain, where *sofrito* is one of the fundamental preparations in Spanish cuisine, indispensable in the early stages of cooking paella. The ingredients for *sofrito* vary with each recipe. In Spain the basic ingredients are tomato, olive oil and garlic.

Sofritos vary greatly from one region to another. The best-known varieties are Catalan *sofrito* (olive oil, onion, tomato and picada, an aromatic mixture pounded to a paste in a mortar using a pestle, see page 56), Valencian *sofrito* (puréed fresh tomatoes, olive oil and chopped garlic), and Alicante *sofrito* (olive oil, garlic, ñora peppers and fresh tomatoes cooked with shellfish).

Sofrito can be made in large quantities because it keeps well in the refrigerator for 3–4 days and can be used in other recipes. It is also suitable for freezing in portions. If you do not have time to make a *sofrito*, a commercially prepared tomato passata (puréed canned tomatoes) can be used, but the results will not be as good as with fresh, home-made puréed tomatoes.

SOME BASIC TECHNIQUES

HOW TO GRATE FRESH TOMATOES
Choose tomatoes that are fully ripened. Halve the tomatoes and, using a teaspoon, scoop out and discard the seeds. Grate the flesh of each half over a bowl until only the skin is left in your hand; discard the skin.

HOW TO PURÉE FRESH TOMATO
Plunge the tomatoes into boiling water for a few seconds until the skin loosens and starts to split; remove with a slotted spoon. The length of time needed for blanching will depend on how firm or how ripe the tomatoes are. Some varieties can be peeled with no blanching at all. Halve, remove the seeds with a teaspoon and purée the flesh in a blender, food grinder or food processor.

HOW TO USE SAFFRON FOR PAELLA
In Valencia, where paella originates, powdered flavourless colouring agents are used. For me, however, it is essential to use saffron because of its unique flavour. Allow a pinch of saffron threads per person. Preheat the oven to 150°C/300°F/Gas Mark 2. Wrap the saffron in an aluminium foil parcel and place in the oven for 30 seconds until lightly toasted. The threads should have hardened, but they must not be allowed to burn. Carefully unwrap the parcel and tip the saffron threads into a mortar. Using a pestle, pound to a fine powder. This will be dissolved in a little hot stock before being added to the rice, usually halfway through the paella's cooking time. You can omit this process, if desired, by using ground saffron, but be sure to use high-quality saffron powder if choosing this option.

SOFRITO DE TOMATE
TOMATO SOFRITO

Preparation time: 25 minutes
Cooking time: 50 minutes
Makes about 500 ml (2¼ cups)

50 ml (¼ cup) olive oil

¼ red onion, finely chopped

¼ Spanish onion, finely chopped

½ shallot, finely chopped

1 clove garlic, finely chopped

¼ green bell pepper, seeded and cut into fine strips

¼ carrot, cut into fine strips

¼ white part of a leek, cut into fine strips

100 ml (scant ½ cup) dry white wine

500 g (1 lb 2 oz) very ripe tomatoes, diced, or canned peeled whole plum (roma) tomatoes, roughly diced

1 sprig rosemary

1 bay leaf

pinch of sugar

salt and pepper

An aromatic, flavoursome mixture cooked in olive oil, sofrito is the first stage of cooking paella. This recipe is for a versatile everyday sofrito and can also be used for many other recipes. Sofrito can be frozen in smaller batches to keep on hand ready for use.

Heat the oil in a large pan over low heat and gently sauté the onions until starting to soften (do not allow them to colour). Add the shallot and sauté until it is also softened and translucent, then add the garlic and cook until the garlic is opaque. Next, add the bell pepper, carrot and leek, and continue sautéing over low heat until these have softened and disintegrated.

When the mixture has thickened, pour in the white wine and use to deglaze the pan, scraping up any bits on the bottom with a wooden spatula. When the alcohol has evaporated, add the tomatoes, rosemary and bay leaf. Simmer very gently over very low heat for 50 minutes, stirring occasionally. Season with salt and pepper, and add a pinch of sugar to counteract the acidity of the tomatoes. Remove the bay leaf and rosemary.

Pass the mixture through a food or vegetable mill over a bowl, then push through a fine-mesh sieve or chinois, pressing it through well. It is not advisable to use a blender or food processor for this process because this incorporates air into the mixture and alters the colour of the sofrito. Taste and add more salt or sugar if needed. Allow to cool, then store in the refrigerator in a tightly sealed container.

SOFRITO DE TOMATE 2
TOMATO SOFRITO NO. 2

Preparation time: 20 minutes
Cooking time: 50 minutes
Makes about 600 ml (2½ cups)

◉ →

200 ml (scant 1 cup) olive oil

2 red onions, finely chopped

4 cloves garlic, finely chopped

800 g (1¾ lb) very ripe tomatoes, peeled, seeded and diced

pinch of sugar

salt and pepper

Ideally, very sweet, violet-tinged Figueres red onions should be used for this recipe, but it also works well with ordinary red onions. This sofrito is widely used in Catalonia, where it is usually prepared separately.

Put the olive oil and onions in a large pan over low heat and sauté until soft and translucent. Add the garlic and cook until the garlic is opaque and starting to colour. Tip in the tomatoes. Stir through and simmer over low heat until the sofrito has thickened considerably (this will take about 50 minutes). Season with salt and pepper and add a pinch of sugar to counteract the acidity of the tomatoes.

Pass the mixture through a food or vegetable mill (do not use a blender or food processor, to avoid introducing air). Allow to cool completely. Store in a tightly sealed container in the refrigerator.

SOFRITO DE TOMATE CON PICADA Y BOGAVANTE
TOMATO AND LOBSTER SOFRITO WITH PICADA

Makes about 350 ml (1½ cups)
Preparation time: 30 minutes
Cooking time: 15 minutes

1 uncooked lobster head

100 ml (scant ½ cup) olive oil

3 cloves garlic

5 hazelnuts

1 dried ñora pepper, stalk removed and seeded, coarsely crumbled

2 sprigs of flat-leaf parsley

8 saffron threads, toasted and pounded

200 ml (scant 1 cup) Tomato Sofrito no. 2 (page 54)

salt and pepper

This variation on the classic Catalan sofrito is as popular as the preceding recipe. An aromatic and flavoursome paste made by pounding the ingredients in a mortar with a pestle is added to the thickened tomato purée. This recipe is ideal for two servings of lobster paella, hence the presence of the lobster head in the ingredients.

Remove and discard the leathery stomach sac from the centre of the lobster's head. Scrape all the contents of the lobster head away from the shell: these will give the sofrito its lobster flavour. Where necessary, cut the contents into small pieces.

To make the picada, pour the oil into a large pan over low heat. Add the garlic, hazelnuts, ñora pepper and parsley, and gently sauté for about 10 minutes until lightly browned. Transfer to a mortar, leaving the oil behind in the pan. Add the toasted saffron threads to the mortar, and pound the mixture to a smooth, homogenous paste with the pestle. Set aside. Cook the contents of the lobster's head gently in the oil left in the pan until very lightly browned. Remove from the heat; tip up the pan on an angle and use a spoon to remove the oil, leaving all the lobster solids and juices behind. Add the paste from the mortar to the contents of the pan. Stir well before pushing through a fine-mesh sieve or chinois; use a wooden spoon to press as much of the mixture as possible through the sieve. Taste and season with salt and pepper if desired.

PICADA
PICADA

Makes 2 tablespoons
Preparation time: 25 minutes

500 ml (2¼ cups) olive oil

6 hazelnuts, skinned

1 clove garlic

1 dried ñora pepper, stalk removed and seeded, coarsely crumbled

¼ teaspoon saffron threads, toasted and pounded

1 sprig of flat-leaf parsley

1 tablespoon sherry vinegar

The preparation of picada is described in the Tomato and Lobster Sofrito recipe (above), but a full recipe is given here by itself. It's an essential technique of Catalan cooking, and consists of pounding together several ingredients with fat-rich nuts, such as hazelnuts or almonds, in a mortar, and adding it to the dish during cooking. This picada was designed for a meat-based paella made with pork, and is enough for 2 people.

Heat the olive oil in a pan and fry the hazelnuts until lightly browned. Remove them and set to one side. In the same oil fry the garlic until it is golden and set aside with the hazelnuts.

Still using the same oil (add some more if necessary), fry the ñora pepper until it starts to release its aroma, but without allowing it to burn. Remove from the heat. Combine all the ingredients in the mortar and pound until a smooth paste is obtained, which can then be diluted with a little of the cooking liquid from the paella.

OLIVAS FOGÓN
FOGÓN-STYLE OLIVES

Makes 1 kg (2¼ lb)
Preparation time: 10 minutes, + 1 hour
for drying
Cooking time: 3 hours

1 kg (2¼ lb) pitted black olives, drained

1 unwaxed orange

1 unwaxed lime

2 sprigs of rosemary

2 sprigs of lemon thyme

2 lemongrass stalks, bruised

1 sprig of flat-leaf parsley

15 g (½ oz) fresh ginger

1 teaspoon black peppercorns

1 teaspoon coriander seeds

1 sprig of basil

2 cloves garlic

500 ml (2¼ cups) olive oil

These olives can be served with apéritifs (or at any time of your choosing), or you can include them in various recipes, such as in sauces, for stuffing chickens, to accompany fish or oven-baked potatoes.

Preheat the oven to 100°C/200°F/Gas Mark ½. Spread out the olives in a layer on a lipped baking sheet, and part-dry in the oven for 1 hour.

Zest the orange and lime using a vegetable peeler, taking care to avoid any white pith. Mix together all the ingredients in a large bowl, and place in hot, sterilized preserving jars. Seal the jars, place in a roasting pan and carefully fill the pan with hot water so that it comes up the sides of the jars. Transfer to the oven and cook very gently for 3 hours. The water should barely simmer and should not boil. Remove from the oven and allow to cool completely.

CONDIMENTO DE LIMÓN
LEMON RELISH

Makes 1 litre (4¼ cups)
Preparation time: 30 minutes
Cooking time: about 1 hour

unwaxed lemons

0 g (¼ cup) sugar

This lemon relish keeps well if stored in the refrigerator in an airtight container. It can be used for all kinds of recipes, such as vinaigrettes and sauces.

Wash and dry the lemons. Peel using a vegetable peeler, removing only the zest and none of the white pith. Chop the zest very finely. Add the zest to a large non-reactive pan filled with cold water and bring to a boil. Drain. Repeat these last two steps five times, using fresh water each time.

Squeeze the lemons to extract all their juice. Put the lemon juice and sugar in a non-reactive pan. Bring to a boil and continue boiling until the liquid has reduced by half. Stir the zest into the lemon syrup, and allow to reduce over low heat until a consistency similar to jam is reached. Pot into a hot, sterilized jar with a tight-fitting lid, seal and label. Allow to cool completely.

FLAVOURED OILS

An important stage in the preparation of paella involves heating and stirring the rice in flavoured olive oil until all the rice grains are translucent, before adding the stock or other liquid. This process impregnates the grains with the flavours of the *sofrito* and prevents the rice from sticking, so it is a good idea to use appropriately flavoured oil for each paella recipe. If you do not have time to prepare these flavoured oils, you can simply use olive oil instead.

When these oils are made with perishable ingredients (seafood, fish and so on), they will only keep for two or three days in the refrigerator, so you will not be making a sizeable quantity. However, they can also be used for other dishes. If made with less perishable products, such as dried fruit, ham, garlic and aromatic herbs, they keep for longer and can also be used for other recipes.

To capture fully the flavour of the ingredients, I prefer to use a mild oil, such as sunflower or grapeseed oil. Neutral-tasting oils retain the flavour of the ingredients cooked in them more effectively.

When browning ingredients in the pan in which they are to be cooked, the oil of choice has traditionally been olive oil. Cornicabra olive oil is the most suitable oil for this purpose because it tolerates heat well. Once it is heated to temperatures above 60°–70°C (140°–150°F), however, olive oil loses some of its flavour and aroma, so there is no need to use the best-quality oil for cooking at high temperatures.

Flavoured oils can be made by one of two methods: first, by infusing cold olive oil, which can be left in the refrigerator for up to 2 months to macerate. The oil will taste of itself and of the chosen flavouring. Another, quicker method consists of putting the flavourings (garlic, herbs, spices) in a suitable receptacle, pouring in the oil and placing it in a microwave oven on the defrost setting for 30 minutes, without heating it. Repeat this procedure two or three times.

ACEITE DE AJO
GARLIC OIL

Makes about 1 litre (4¼ cups)
Preparation time: 15 minutes
Infusion time: 2 months or 2 hours
(depending on your chosen method)

**200 g (7 oz) garlic, halved lengthwise
and central shoots removed**

**1 litre (4½ cups) Cornicabra olive oil or
any good-quality extra virgin olive oil**

*This oil can also be used for other purposes, such as cooking fish,
in vinaigrettes, and for frying.*

Put the garlic in a sterilized opaque jar or container with an
airtight seal. Pour in the oil, seal tightly and let macerate in the
refrigerator for 2 months until the oil is infused with the flavour
of the garlic.

Alternatively, use the quick microwave method. Prepare the garlic
and place in the container as described above. Pour in the oil, and
put the unsealed container in a microwave oven on the defrost
setting for 30 minutes without heating. Repeat this procedure two
or three times. Seal tightly and store in the refrigerator.

ACEITE DE CÍTRICOS
CITRUS-FLAVOURED OIL

Makes about 1 litre (4¼ cups)
Preparation time: 15 minutes
Infusion time: 2 months or 2 hours
(depending on your chosen method)

**8 lemongrass stalks, tough outer layers
removed, bruised and finely chopped**

**100 g (1 cup) fresh ginger, peeled and
cut into fine strips**

**3 tablespoons freeze-dried green
peppercorns**

4 tablespoons coriander seeds

20 peppermint leaves

zest of 2 oranges

zest of 5 limes

**1 litre (4¼ cups) olive oil (use first
cold pressing)**

Put all the flavourings and aromatics in a sterilized jar or container with an airtight seal. Pour in the oil, seal tightly and store
in the refrigerator for 2 months to allow the flavours to infuse
the oil.

Alternatively, use the quick microwave method. Fill the container
as described above, but do not seal. Put the unsealed container in
a microwave oven on the defrost setting for 30 minutes, without
heating, and repeat this process two or three times. Seal tightly
and store in the refrigerator.

ACEITE DE JENGIBRE
GINGER OIL

Makes about 1 litre (4¼ cups)
Preparation time: 20 minutes
Infusion time: 2 months or 2 hours
(depending on your chosen method)

**500 g (1 lb 2 oz) fresh ginger, peeled
and grated**

**1 litre (4¼ cups) olive oil (use first
cold pressing)**

Put the ginger in a sterilized container with an airtight seal. Pour
in the oil, seal and store in the refrigerator for 2 months.

Alternatively, use the microwave method. Fill the container, but
do not seal. Put the unsealed container in a microwave oven on
the defrost setting for 30 minutes and repeat this process two or
three times. Seal tightly and store in the refrigerator.

ACEITE DE HONGOS
MUSHROOM OIL

Makes about 1 litre (4¼ cups)
Preparation time: 15 minutes
Infusion time: 2 months or 2 hours
(depending on your chosen method)

**300 g (11 oz) uncooked fresh
mushrooms, cleaned, or trimmings
from uncooked fresh mushrooms**

**1 litre (4¼ cups) olive oil (first
cold pressing)**

*The oil can be made with any type of fresh mushroom, such as fresh
ceps (porcini) when in season.*

Rinse and drain the mushrooms or mushroom trimmings, making
sure that there is no earth or grit left on them. Pat dry thoroughly
with paper towels, and put in a sterilized container. Pour in the oil,
seal tightly and store in the refrigerator for 2 months.

Alternatively, put the unsealed container in a microwave oven on
the defrost setting for 30 minutes and repeat this operation two or
three times. Seal tightly and store in the refrigerator.

ACEITE DE SARDINAS
SARDINE OIL

Makes about 500 ml (2¼ cups)
Preparation time: 20 minutes
Cooking time: 15 minutes

**250 g (9 oz) uncooked sardine
bones and heads**

500 ml (2¼ cups) sunflower oil

This oil will keep for up to 4 days in the refrigerator.

Rinse the sardine bones and heads thoroughly, and place in a bowl.
Leave the bowl under cold running water, left to run slowly over
the bones until the water runs completely clear. Drain them.

Put the bones and heads in a pan, pour the oil over them and
heat slowly. Gently sauté over low heat for 15 minutes until lightly
browned. Remove from the heat, drain off the oil and discard
the bones. Carefully strain the oil through a fine-mesh sieve into
a sterilized container. Allow to cool. Store in the refrigerator.

ACEITE DE GAMBAS
PRAWN (SHRIMP) OIL

Makes about 600 ml (2½ cups)
Preparation time: 10 minutes
Cooking time: 15 minutes

250 g (9 oz) prawn (shrimp) heads

400 ml (1¾ cups) sunflower oil

This oil will keep for up to 4 days if stored in the refrigerator.

Put the prawn (shrimp) heads in a pan, and pour the cold oil over
them. Heat slowly and gently sauté the prawn heads over low
heat for 15 minutes until lightly browned. Remove from the heat,
and drain off the oil into a measuring jug (large measuring cup)
or similar; discard the heads. Carefully strain the oil through a fine-
mesh sieve or chinois into a sterilized jar or container with an
airtight seal. Allow to cool. Store in the refrigerator.

ACEITE DE BOGAVANTE O LANGOSTA
LOBSTER OIL

Makes about 500 ml (2¼ cups)
Preparation time: 10 minutes
Cooking time: 30 minutes

2 uncooked lobster heads

500 ml (2¼ cups) sunflower oil

This oil will keep for a few days in the refrigerator. You can add spices or herbs to it, according to your taste.

Put the lobster shells and heads in a pan, cover them with the cold oil and heat slowly. Gently sauté over low heat for 30 minutes until lightly browned. Remove from the heat and drain off the oil; discard the shells and heads. Carefully strain the oil through a fine-mesh sieve or chinois into a sterilized jar or container with an airtight seal. Allow to cool. Store in the refrigerator.

ACEITE DE CIGALAS
LANGOUSTINE OIL

Makes about 400 ml (1¾ cups)
Preparation time: 2 hours 10 minutes
Cooking time: 30 minutes

◎ →

250 g (9 oz) langoustine heads and claws, rinsed thoroughly

400 ml (1¾ cups) sunflower oil

This oil will keep for a few days in the refrigerator and can be used for cooking fish, in sauces and to make mayonnaise.

Put the langoustine heads and claws in a pan, pour the oil over them and heat slowly. Gently sauté over low heat for 30 minutes until golden brown. Remove from the heat and drain off the oil; discard the heads and claws. Carefully strain the oil through a fine-mesh sieve or chinois into a sterilized jar or container with an airtight seal. Allow to cool. Store in the refrigerator.

ACEITE DE JAMÓN IBÉRICO
IBÉRICO HAM-FLAVOURED OIL

Makes about 400 ml (1¾ cups)
Preparation time: 5 minutes
Infusion time: 2 months or 2 hours
(depending on your chosen method)

200 g (7 oz) Ibérico ham fat

400 ml (1¾ cups) sunflower oil

When preparing this flavoured oil, you need to use the unsaturated fat of the ham, which is a pinkish colour; do not use the oxidized, brownish fat.

To use the quick microwave method, fill the container with the ham fat and oil, but do not seal. Put the unsealed jar or container in a microwave oven on the defrost setting for 30 minutes and repeat this process two or three times. Seal tightly and store in the refrigerator until needed.

Alternatively, put the fat in a sterilized container with an airtight seal. Pour in the oil, seal tightly and store in the refrigerator for 2 months to allow the flavours to infuse the oil.

PAELLAS ON THE STOVE

THE EIGHT STAGES OF MAKING PAELLA RICE

I have subdivided the preparation of paella rice into eight stages in order to provide a step-by-step guide. My aim is to help readers, no matter what their level of experience, to organize the way they follow my recipes when making paella rice. Once this basic method has been mastered, much greater freedom and creativity in the kitchen is possible. For example, you may choose not to fry the rice until it is translucent, opting instead to sprinkle it by hand directly into the boiling stock in the pan, ending up with a slightly different dish.

Of course, the procedure will differ depending on whether you are working in your kitchen (on the stove top and in the oven) or outdoors, on a barbecue. Listed below are the eight stages for indoor cooking.

Preheat the oven to 150°C/300°F/Gas Mark 2. Heat the oil in the paella pan over low heat, add a few flavourings, such as ñora pepper and garlic, sauté gently until they are lightly browned and remove them from the pan. Put them into a mortar with a little stock and reduce them to a paste with a pestle. Alternatively, put the browned flavourings with a little stock into a food processor and process to a paste.

Add the basic ingredients, such as poultry, meat, fish and seafood, to the pan. If the recipe includes seafood that only needs a short cooking time, sauté it briefly for a few minutes until very lightly browned and remove it from the pan. Add the seafood to the paella at the end of the cooking time.

②

Once any liquid has evaporated, add the rice and cook over low heat for a few minutes, stirring with a wooden spatula, until thoroughly coated and translucent; do not allow the rice to burn. At this point, deglaze the pan by pouring wine or another type of alcohol into it, scraping up any bits on the bottom of the pan with a wooden spatula.

③

Add the ñora and garlic paste to the pan. Add the tomatoes, prepared separately, or passata (puréed canned tomatoes) and allow to cook for a few minutes until the mixture has reduced and thickened.

Add the paprika, stir through and cook over moderate heat for a few seconds, watching it carefully.

④

Add the hot liquid (usually stock). To ensure the boiling point is reached immediately, the liquid must be very hot before adding it. This will help you to be more accurate with the cooking time.

⑤

Add the toasted and ground saffron threads and allow to boil rapidl For exact timing, set a timer for 17 minutes when you add the saffron. Taste and season with salt to taste. From this moment on, the seasoning can no longer be adjusted.

⑥

After 5 minutes you will start to see the ingredients come together. From this moment on nothing can be added. Reduce the heat to moderate and allow to simmer.

⑦

Two minutes later the rice will start to swell and rise above the surface of the liquid. Transfer the paella to the preheated oven and cook for 12 minutes.

⑧

Take the paella out of the oven. If you have set aside any ingredients at an earlier stage, add them 2–3 minutes before the end of the oven cooking time. Allow the paella to cook for a further 2–3 minutes and remove it from the oven. Let the paella rest for 3 minutes, then check if the rice is cooked; it should be tender but very slightly firm to the bite. If it has not quite finished cooking, cover it with a sheet of aluminium foil. Alternatively, if some liquid is left over, allow it to evaporate.

IF YOU HAVE NO OVEN

You can cook entirely on the stove, providing the heat is evenly distributed underneath the paella pan (see below). It is important to allow the paella to rest for a few minutes once the cooking time is up.

Follow steps 1–6 as above, then proceed as follows:

⑦

Instead of putting the paella in the oven, reduce the heat to a very low heat and allow to simmer until the liquid has completely evaporated. If your pan is larger than the ring or burner beneath it, continue cooking by placing it over two rings or burners, partially rotating it at regular intervals so that the contents cook evenly.

⑧

Cover the entire paella with a clean, damp dish towel. Remove from the heat and allow to rest for 3 minutes, then check if the rice is cooked; it should be tender but very slightly firm to the bite. If it has not quite finished cooking, cover it with a sheet of aluminium foil.

PAELLA RICE 'A BANDA'

Serves 2
Preparation time: 30 minutes
(excluding fumet)
Cooking time: 17 minutes

For the fumet

1 kg (2¼ lb) whole rock fish such as red mullet, gurnard (sea robin) or scorpion fish, cleaned, scaled and gills removed

150 g (5 oz) uncooked prawns (shrimp)

200 g (7 oz) shore (green) crabs or small swimming (blue) crabs

100 ml (scant ½ cup) extra-virgin olive oil

1 potato, diced

1 leek, cut into fine strips

1 carrot, cut into fine strips

1 celery stalk, cut into fine strips

100 g (3½ oz) fennel bulb, finely sliced

1 onion, finely sliced

2 cloves garlic, finely chopped

1 bay leaf

1 small sprig of rosemary

1 small stick of liquorice

1 star anise

For the paella rice

1 dried ñora pepper, stalk removed and seeded

4 king prawns (jumbo shrimp)

4 langoustines

100 ml (scant ½ cup) olive oil

1 clove garlic, finely chopped

100 g (3½ oz) cuttlefish, white part (mantle) only, cleaned and cut into 1-cm (½-inch) dice

200 g (1 cup) bomba or other short-grain rice

1 large tomato, halved, seeded and grated, skin discarded

1 teaspoon Spanish sweet smoked paprika

¼ teaspoon saffron threads, toasted and pounded

salt and pepper

A banda *means 'next to' in Spanish: the fish and shellfish (the* banda) *used to make the fumet are served separately, while the rice is cooking. I suggest serving them at this stage, but you can also keep them warm under aluminium foil and serve them at the same time as the rice.*

This paella can be served with Aioli (page 36). For a moist texture, use a 30-cm (12-inch) paella pan suitable for use on the stove and in the oven.

The day before preparing the fumet, put the ñora peppers in a bowl of cold water and let soak overnight. The following day, drain the peppers, and scrape the flesh away from the skins with a knife. Discard the skin and reserve the flesh. The following day make the fumet, following the instructions for the Rock Fish Fumet on page 36. You will need no more than 600 ml (2½ cups) of fumet for this recipe, so any left-over fumet can be used for another recipe.

Preheat the oven to 150°C/300°F/Gas Mark 2. Remove the heads from the king prawns (jumbo shrimp) and langoustines, scoop out the creamy contents and set aside in a bowl. Peel the king prawns and langoustines and set aside. Rather than using the reserved shellfish heads for the fumet, I prefer to fry them in the paella pan to brown them lightly, and in this way they give their unique flavour to the sofrito.

Recipe continues over

PAELLA RICE 'A BANDA'

1. Heat the oil in the paella pan over low heat, then add the ñora pepper and garlic. Sauté gently until lightly brown, taking care not to burn them, and as soon as they release their aroma, take them out of the pan and set aside. Add the cuttlefish and the reserved contents of the shellfish heads to the pan. Cook, without allowing them to brown, and stir. Add the king prawns and langoustines and sauté for 1–2 minutes until firm but not fully cooked. Remove them from the pan and set to one side.

2. Allow the liquid produced by the seafood to evaporate in the pan, then add the rice and cook over low heat for a few minutes, stirring with a wooden spatula, until thoroughly coated and translucent; do not allow the rice to burn. Put the ñora pepper and garlic into a mortar and pound with a pestle or crush them with the blade of a large knife.

3. Stir the crushed pepper and garlic into the rice, add the tomato and allow to cook for a few minutes until the mixture has reduced and thickened. Add the paprika, stir through and cook over moderate for a few seconds, taking care that it does not burn.

4. Once it is all well mixed, pour in the very hot fumet and deglaze the pan, scraping up any bits on the bottom of the pan with a wooden spatula.

5. Add the saffron and a little salt. Spread the rice out evenly to cover the bottom of the paella pan. Bring to a boil and, if you have a timer, set it for 17 minutes. Cook over medium-high heat.

6. After 5 minutes, reduce the heat to moderate. The rice should have risen to the surface of the liquid. Taste the fumet and add a little salt, if necessary, bearing in mind that the flavours will become more pronounced as the liquid evaporates. Remove the shellfish heads.

7. Transfer the paella to the preheated oven. After 12 minutes it will be ready.

8. Take the paella out of the oven, allow it to rest for 3 minutes, then serve.

EXTRA-FINE PAELLA RICE 'A BANDA' WITHOUT THE 'BANDA'

Serves 2
Preparation time: 20 minutes
(excluding fumet)
Cooking time: 17 minutes

500 ml (2 cups) Fish Fumet (page 48)

**100 ml (scant ½ cup) Garlic Oil
(page 60) or ordinary olive oil**

**200 g (7 oz) cuttlefish, white part
(mantle) only, cleaned and cut into
1-cm (½-inch) dice**

**200 g (7 oz) small squid, cleaned
and diced**

**200 g (1 cup) bomba or other short-
grain rice**

**150 ml (⅔ cups) Tomato Sofrito
(page 54)**

**½ teaspoon Spanish sweet
smoked paprika**

**¼ teaspoon saffron threads, toasted
and pounded**

salt

This recipe is my own personal interpretation of the traditional Paella Rice 'a Banda' (page 68). When you put this paella in the oven, always make sure that there is an even, thin layer of rice completely covering the bottom of the paella pan. Although this layer of rice is thin, it should hide the bottom of the pan completely.

The rice should be served without the banda (the seafood used to make the fumet) in the paella pan, not on plates, and if possible with a wooden spoon. Each person should start by detaching the rice from around the edges of the pan. This crunchy rice has a very pronounced, caramelized taste that brings out the flavour of the seafood.

For an extra-fine texture, use a 41-cm (16-inch) paella pan suitable for use on the stove and in the oven.

Before starting the recipe, heat the Fish Fumet but do not allow it to boil. Preheat the oven to 150°C/300°F/Gas Mark 2. Heat the Garlic Oil in the paella pan, then add the cuttlefish and small squid. Sauté for a few minutes, without allowing them to colour, stirring continuously. Add the rice to the pan and cook over low heat for a few minutes, stirring with a wooden spatula, until thoroughly coated and translucent; do not allow the rice to burn.

Pour in the Tomato Sofrito and stir the ingredients well. Deglaze the pan, scraping up any bits on the bottom of the pan with a wooden spatula. Add the paprika, stir through and cook over moderate heat for a few seconds, then pour in the very hot Fish Fumet.

Add the saffron and stir. Add a little salt and spread the rice out evenly to cover the bottom of the paella pan, levelling it out with the back of a wooden spoon. Bring to a boil and, if you have a timer, set it for 17 minutes. Taste and season with salt to taste if necessary. Leave to cook over very high heat.

After 5 minutes, the rice should rise to the surface of the liquid. Make sure the rice is evenly distributed in the pan and transfer it to the preheated oven.

After 12 minutes, remove the paella from the oven, allow it to rest for 3 minutes, then serve.

BLACK PAELLA RICE WITH CUTTLEFISH INK

Serves 2
Preparation time: 15 minutes
(excluding fumet and stock)
Cooking time: 17 minutes

100 ml (scant ½ cup) Garlic Oil
(page 60) or ordinary olive oil

200 g (7 oz) monkfish tail, diced into
1.5-cm (¾-inch) pieces

200 g (7 oz) cuttlefish, washed and
diced into 1-cm (½-inch) pieces

200 g (1 cup) bomba or other short-
grain rice

200 g (scant 1 cup) Black Stock (page 45)

½ teaspoon Spanish sweet
smoked paprika

400 ml (1¾ cups) Fish Fumet (page 48)

50 g (1 cup) spring onions (scallions),
green part only, sliced into thin rings,
or spinach stalks, finely chopped

salt

I first tasted this dish at my restaurant in Cuenca: Mesón Nelia. It was prepared by José Navarro, a chef who comes from Ainsa, in the Pyrenean part of Aragon, northern Spain, and whose cooking has been influenced by Ibizan cuisine. He taught me to serve it with a salad of raw, peeled green bell peppers simply dressed with olive oil and sherry vinegar. This salad complements the rice to perfection and cleanses the palate between mouthfuls of paella, enabling you to taste the rice properly each time. This paella should not be confused with the black rice of Ampurdán (Catalonia), a traditional recipe that is not made with cuttlefish ink but with slow-cooked onions, which turn the rice very dark, almost black.

At Fogón I devised a variation on this recipe for the actress Maria de Medeiros and her husband Augustin, 'partners in crime' and patrons of the restaurant. As a true Catalan, Augustin likes to have Aioli (page 36) with his paella. So, three minutes before the rice is cooked, I spread a thin layer of Aioli (1 cm/½ inch) over the entire surface of the paella, then put it back in the oven until it forms a nice crisp and attractive golden crust. The rice is served directly from the pan at the table.

For a moist texture, use a 34-cm (13½-inch) paella pan suitable for use on the stove and in the oven.

Preheat the oven to 150°C/300°F/Gas Mark 2. Heat the Garlic Oil in the paella pan over low heat. Add the monkfish and cuttlefish and sauté gently. When all the liquid from the fish has evaporated, push the fish towards the edge of the pan. Add the rice into the centre and cook over low heat for a few minutes, stirring with a wooden spatula, until thoroughly cooked and translucent; do not allow the rice to burn.

Add the Black Stock and stir the ingredients well, deglazing the pan by scraping up any bits on the bottom of the pan with a wooden spatula. Add the paprika, stir through and cook over moderate heat for a few seconds, taking care that it does not burn. Pour in the very hot Fish Fumet. Season with salt and spread the rice out evenly to cover the bottom of the paella pan completely.

Bring to a boil. If you have a timer, set it for 17 minutes. Cook for 5 minutes until the rice rises to the surface of the liquid. Taste the stock and season again with salt if necessary, bearing in mind that the flavours will become more pronounced as the liquid evaporates.

Spread the rice out evenly again in the pan and cook in the preheated oven for 12 minutes. Remove the paella from the oven and allow it to rest for 2 minutes. Sprinkle the surface with the sliced spring onion or spinach stalks and serve immediately.

PAELLA RICE WITH MONKFISH, SPINACH AND ARTICHOKES

Serves 2
Preparation time: 30 minutes
(excluding fumet)
Cooking time: 17 minutes

**600 ml (2½ cups) monkfish fumet
(see Fish Fumet, page 48, and use
monkfish bones and trimmings or
a monkfish head)**

4 very young, fresh artichokes

1 lemon, quartered

50 ml (¼ cup) olive oil

**150 g (5 oz) tomatoes, halved, seeded
and grated, skin discarded**

300 g (11 oz) monkfish, diced

**150 g (5 oz) spinach, washed, patted
dry, stalks removed and reserved**

**200 g (7 oz) spring onions (scallions),
cut into fine strips**

1 clove garlic, finely chopped

**200 g (1 cup) bomba or other short-
grain rice**

**½ teaspoon Spanish sweet
smoked paprika**

**¼ teaspoon saffron threads, toasted
and pounded**

salt

*The spinach and artichokes react with the metal of the paella pan
and become oxidized, and, far from being a fault, this is highly
sought after (see Introduction, page 12).*

*A variation on the standard method of preparation is to cook the
spinach very rapidly in a frying pan or skillet over high heat and
to add it at the same time as the saffron. This results in it being
slightly less cooked.*

*For a moist texture, use a 34-cm (13½-inch) paella pan suitable for
use on the stove and in the oven.*

Heat the monkfish fumet but do not allow it to boil. Preheat the
oven to 150°C/300°F/Gas Mark 2.

Clean the artichokes, trim the tops and cut off the sharp tips of
the leaves; remove the hairy choke if there is one. Rub lemon
quarters over all the cut surfaces to prevent discoloration. Set the
artichokes aside in a bowl of water acidulated with lemon juice.

Heat 1 tablespoon of the olive oil in a frying pan or skillet over
low heat, add the grated tomato and sauté until reduced and
thickened. Heat the remaining olive oil in the paella pan and sauté
the monkfish until lightly browned. Add the vegetables and cook
over moderate heat for 2 minutes. Add the garlic to the centre of
the pan and cook very briefly until lightly browned.

Add the rice and cook over low heat for a few minutes, stirring
with a wooden spatula, until thoroughly coated and translucent;
do not allow the rice to burn. Add the fried tomato and stir with a
spatula until all the ingredients are well mixed.

Add the paprika, stir through and cook over moderate heat for
a few seconds, but do not allow it to burn. Pour in the hot monkfish
fumet, stir and bring to a boil. Add the saffron. If you have a timer,
set it to 17 minutes. Cook over high heat for 5 minutes until the
rice rises to the surface of the liquid. Taste and season with salt
if necessary, bearing in mind that the flavours will become more
pronounced as the liquid evaporates.

Put the paella in the preheated oven. While it is cooking, finely
chop the spinach stalks. Remove the paella from the oven after
12 minutes. Allow to rest for 3 minutes, then sprinkle the chopped
spinach stalks over the paella. They will add a note of acidity and
freshness to the dish.

ARROZ EN PAELLA CON ATÚN, VERDURAS, GARBANZOS Y PASAS
PAELLA RICE WITH TUNA, VEGETABLES, CHICKPEAS AND SULTANAS (GOLDEN RAISINS)

Serves 2
Preparation time: 25 minutes
(excluding stock)
Cooking time: 17 minutes

400 ml (1¾ cups) Bonito Stock
(page 40)

50 ml (¼ cup) olive oil

1 dried ñora pepper, stalk and seeds
removed, coarsely crumbled

1 clove garlic

400 g (14 oz) belly or loin cuts of
fresh tuna

100 g (3½ oz) spring onions (scallions),
white parts cut into fine strips, green
parts reserved to garnish

1 red bell pepper, seeded, peeled and
cut into fine strips

1 green bell pepper, seeded, peeled
and cut into fine strips

200 g (1 cup) bomba or other short-
grain rice

100 g (⅓ cup) Tomato Sofrito (page 54)
or passata

½ teaspoon Spanish sweet
smoked paprika

1 tablespoon sultanas (golden raisins)

0 g (⅓ cup) cooked chickpeas

¼ teaspoon saffron threads, toasted
and pounded

salt

For a moist texture, use a 34-cm (13½-inch) paella pan suitable for use on the stove and in the oven.

Heat the Bonito Stock but do not allow it to boil. Preheat the oven to 150°C/300°F/Gas Mark 2.

Heat the oil in the paella pan over low heat. Add the ñora pepper and garlic and sauté gently. When they release their aroma, take them out of the pan, put them into a mortar and pound to a paste with the pestle.

Add the tuna to the paella pan and cook briefly for a few minutes, until lightly browned all over, then remove it from the pan and set aside, covered with a sheet of aluminium foil.

Add the white part of the spring onions and the bell pepper strips to the paella pan and cook over moderate heat for a few minutes, until they have softened. Add the rice and cook over low heat for a few minutes, stirring with a wooden spoon, until thoroughly cooked and translucent; do not allow the rice to burn. Add the Tomato Sofrito and stir the ingredients well, deglazing the pan by scraping up any bits on the bottom of the pan with a wooden spatula. Once the tomato has thickened, add the paprika and cook gently over low heat for a few seconds, taking care that it does not burn.

Add the hot stock, ñora pepper and garlic paste, raisins, chickpeas and saffron. If you have a timer, set it to 17 minutes. Cook over moderate heat for 5 minutes until the rice rises to the surface of the liquid.

Taste the stock and season with salt, if necessary, bearing in mind that the flavours will become more pronounced as the liquid evaporates. Put the paella in the preheated oven for 9 minutes.

Remove the paella from the oven, arrange the tuna on top and return the pan to the oven for 3 minutes. Remove the paella from the oven again and allow to rest for 3 minutes while you slice the green part of the spring onions thinly. Sprinkle these all over the rice and serve.

PAELLA RICE WITH CHICKEN, KING PRAWNS (JUMBO SHRIMP) AND SQUID

Serves 2
Preparation time: 30 minutes
(excluding fumet)
Cooking time: 17 minutes

**400 ml (1¾ cups) Shellfish Fumet
(page 47)**

50 ml (¼ cup) olive oil

1 clove garlic, finely chopped

**6 king prawns (jumbo shrimp),
weighing 30 g (1 oz) each, heads
removed and peeled, with heads and
tails reserved**

**200 g (7 oz) boneless chicken, cut into
30-g (1-oz) pieces**

**200 g (7 oz) squid, cleaned, rinsed and
sliced into rings**

**200 g (1 cup) bomba or other short-
grain rice**

**100 g (⅓ cup) Tomato Sofrito (page 54)
or passata (puréed canned tomatoes)**

**½ teaspoon Spanish sweet
smoked paprika**

**¼ teaspoon saffron threads, toasted
and pounded**

salt

For a moist texture, use a 34-cm (13½-inch) paella pan suitable for use on the stove and in the oven.

Heat the Shellfish Fumet but do not allow it to boil. Preheat the oven to 150°C/300°F/Gas Mark 2.

Heat the olive oil in a paella pan over low heat and fry the garlic gently. Add the prawn (shrimp) tails and sauté for a few minutes over moderate heat until very lightly browned, then set them aside in a dish, covered with a sheet of aluminium foil.

Add the chicken pieces to the pan and sauté for about 5 minutes until browned all over, then push them to the edge of the pan. Put the prawn heads and squid rings into the centre of the pan and cook for a few minutes until all the water they release evaporates.

Add the rice to the pan and cook over low heat for a few minutes, stirring with a wooden spatula, until thoroughly coated and translucent; do not allow the rice to burn. Add the Tomato Sofrito and deglaze the pan, scraping up any bits on the bottom of the pan with a wooden spatula, and stir all the ingredients together.

Add the paprika, sir through and cook over moderate heat for a few seconds, taking care that it does not burn. Pour in the hot Shellfish Fumet and spread out all the ingredients evenly in the pan. Add the saffron. If you have a timer, set it to 17 minutes. Increase the heat, bring to a boil and cook over very high heat for 5 minutes until the rice rises to the surface of the liquid. Take out all the prawn heads with tongs, squeezing them in order to extract all their juices. Taste and season with a little salt, bearing in mind that the flavours will become more pronounced as the liquid evaporates. Put the paella in the preheated oven for 12 minutes.

Remove the paella from the oven, allow it to rest for 3 minutes, then add the prawn tails and serve.

Serves 2
Preparation time: 35 minutes
(excluding fumet)
Cooking time: 17 minutes

600 ml (2½ cups) Fish Fumet (page 48)

150 g (5 oz) large fresh mussels,
well scrubbed and rinsed

50 ml (¼ cup) olive oil

1 clove garlic, finely chopped

200 g (7 oz) boneless chicken, cut into
30-g (1-oz) pieces

2 king prawns (jumbo shrimp), heads
removed and tails peeled

2 langoustines, heads removed and
tails peeled

150 g (5 oz) squid, cleaned and
prepared, cut into rings

monkfish medallions, 70 g (2½ oz)
each

0 g (½ cup) green beans, trimmed and
cut into 3-cm (1¼-inch) lengths

5 g (scant ¼ cup) peas, shelled

green bell pepper, seeded, skinned
and cut into fine strips

00 g (1 cup) bomba or other short-
grain rice

0 g (⅓ cup) Tomato Sofrito (page 54)
passata (puréed canned tomatoes)

teaspoon Spanish sweet
smoked paprika

teaspoon saffron threads, toasted
and pounded

ime

lt

r the mussels

tablespoons olive oil

onion rings

carrots, sliced into rounds

black peppercorns

tablespoons dry white wine

sprigs of flat-leaf parsley

The ingredients of this paella – poultry, fish, shellfish – are served without their bones and shells, which means you could eat it with your eyes shut, hence its name.

For a moist texture, use a 34-cm (13½-inch) paella pan suitable for use on the stove and in the oven.

Heat the Fish Fumet in a paella pan but do not allow it to boil. Preheat the oven to 150°C/300°F/Gas Mark 2.

Put all the ingredients to steam the mussels in a saucepan set over high heat. Add the mussels, cover and cook for a few minutes, shaking the saucepan from time to time, until the mussels open. Take them out of their shells and set them aside in a bowl, without the vegetables, covered with a sheet of aluminium foil.

Heat the oil in the paella pan over low heat and gently sauté the garlic until lightly brown. Add the chicken and sauté for a few minutes until lightly brown all over, then push it towards the edge of the pan. Put the prawn (shrimp) and langoustine heads and tails, the squid and monkfish into the centre of the pan and cook for a few minutes until lightly browned and the liquid from the fish and seafood evaporates. Remove them and set aside. Add the green beans, peas and green bell pepper strips and cook for few minutes until the vegetables have softened.

Add the rice and cook over low heat for a few minutes, stirring with a wooden spatula, until thoroughly coated and translucent; do not allow the rice to burn. Add the Tomato Sofrito and mix well, deglazing the pan by scraping up any bits on the bottom of the pan with a wooden spatula. Add the paprika, stir and cook over moderate heat for a few seconds, taking care that it does not burn.

Pour in the hot stock and stir until combined. Spread the contents of the pan out evenly. Add the saffron and grate lime zest over the surface. If you have a timer, set it to 17 minutes. Bring to a boil and cook over very high heat for 5 minutes, until the rice rises to the surface of the liquid.

Remove the shellfish heads using stainless steel tongs, squeezing well in order to extract all their juice. Taste and season with salt, bearing in mind that the flavours will become more pronounced as the liquid evaporates.

Put the paella in the preheated oven. After 8 minutes, remove it from the oven and arrange the mussels, monkfish, squid, prawns and langoustines over the rice, then return to the oven. After 4 minutes, remove the paella from the oven, allow it to rest for 3 minutes, then serve.

PAELLA RICE WITH MARINATED SWORDFISH

Serves 2
Preparation time:
25 minutes (excluding fumet) +
12 hours marinating
Cooking time: 17 minutes

For the marinade

1 teaspoon Spanish sweet
smoked paprika

1 teaspoon dried oregano

1 teaspoon cumin powder

1 clove garlic, finely chopped

2 tablespoons grated fresh ginger

1 teaspoon ground caraway seeds

½ lime, zest finely grated

200 ml (scant 1 cup) olive oil

1 swordfish, about 300 g (11 oz),
filleted, skin removed and cut into
3-cm (1¼-inch) cubes

For the paella rice

400 ml (1¾ cups) Fish Fumet (page 48)

50 ml (¼ cup) Garlic Oil (page 60) or
ordinary olive oil

2 onions, finely chopped

1 green bell pepper, seeded and cut
into thin strips

200 g (1 cup) bomba or other short-
grain rice

100 g (⅓ cup) Tomato Sofrito (page 54)
or passata (puréed canned tomatoes)

½ teaspoon Spanish sweet
smoked paprika

¼ teaspoon saffron threads, toasted
and pounded

salt

For a moist texture, use a 34-cm (13½-inch) paella pan suitable for use on the stove and in the oven.

The day before, mix the marinade spices and flavourings with the olive oil, stir in the cubes of fish and leave to marinate in the refrigerator for 12 hours in a tightly sealed container.

The following day, drain the pieces of fish on a rack to get rid of as much of the oily marinade as possible. Heat the fumet but do not allow it to boil. Preheat the oven to 150°C/300°F/Gas Mark 2.

Heat the Garlic Oil in the paella pan over low heat, add the marinated swordfish and sauté for a few minutes until lightly browned all over. Remove the fish from the pan and set aside in a deep dish, covered with aluminium foil.

Add the onions and green bell pepper to the paella pan and sauté for a few minutes until softened; do not allow them to brown. Add the rice and cook over low heat for a few minutes, stirring with a wooden spatula, until thoroughly coated and translucent; do not allow the rice to burn. Add the Tomato Sofrito and stir well, deglazing the pan by scraping up any bits on the bottom of the pan with a wooden spatula. Once the mixture has reduced and thickened, add the paprika, stir through and cook over moderate heat for a few seconds, taking care that it does not burn. Pour in the hot fumet, stir and bring to a boil. Add the saffron. If you have a timer, set it to 17 minutes.

Cook over high heat for 5 minutes until the rice rises to the surface of the liquid. Taste the fumet and season with salt, if necessary, bearing in mind that the flavours will become more pronounced as the liquid evaporates. Add the cubes of marinated swordfish.

Put the paella in the preheated oven for 12 minutes. Remove the paella from the oven and allow it to rest for 3 minutes before serving.

BARCELONA-STYLE THURSDAY PAELLA RICE

Serves 10
Preparation time: 40 minutes
(excluding fumet)
Cooking time: 17 minutes

3 litres (13½ cups) Fish Fumet
(page 48)

250 ml (1 cup) olive oil

4 cloves garlic, finely chopped

1 kg (2¼ lb) chicken, deboned and cut
into 30-g (1-oz) pieces

10 king prawns (jumbo shrimp),
heads removed and tails shelled, with
the tails reserved

10 langoustines, heads removed
and tails shelled, with the heads and
tails reserved

10 monkfish fillets, about 70 g (2½ oz)
each

500 g (1 lb 10½ oz) squid, cleaned and
sliced into rings

500 g (1 lb 10½ oz) large fresh
mussels, well scrubbed and cleaned

500 g (1 lb 2 oz) green beans, trimmed
and cut into 3-cm (1¼-inch) lengths

125 g (1 cup) peas, shelled

2 green bell peppers, seeded, skinned
and sliced into thin strips

1 kg (5 cups) bomba or other short-
grain rice

440 ml (2¼ cups) Tomato Sofrito
(page 54) or passata (puréed
canned tomatoes)

2 teaspoons Spanish sweet
smoked paprika

1 teaspoon saffron threads, toasted
and pounded

2 limes

Salt

This paella is made on Thursdays in the bars and neighbourhood restaurants (or casas de comidas) *of Barcelona, where it is often the daily special. It is cooked on a large hotplate and is served straight onto plates.*

Use a metal pan for this recipe (a large baking pan or a large stainless steel gratin dish) large enough for 10 servings and suitable for use on the stove and in the oven.

Heat the Fish Fumet but do not allow it to boil. Preheat the oven to 150°C/300°F/Gas Mark 2. Bring a large pan of water to a boil, add the mussels and cook for 30 seconds, then drain them and set aside.

Heat the oil in the pan over low heat, add the garlic and sauté until lightly browned. Add the chicken pieces and sauté for a few minutes until brown all over, then push them to the edge of the pan. Add the king prawns (jumbo shrimp), langoustines, monkfish and squid and sauté for a few minutes until lightly browned. Remove them from the pan and set aside. Add the green beans, peas and green bell pepper strips to the pan and sauté for a few minutes until the vegetables have softened.

Reduce the heat to low, add the rice and cook for a few minutes, stirring with a wooden spatula, until thoroughly coated and translucent; do not allow the rice to burn. Add the Tomato Sofrito and stir the ingredients well, deglazing the pan by scraping up any bits on the bottom of the pan with a wooden spatula.

Add the smoked paprika, stir through and cook over moderate heat for a few seconds, taking care that it does not burn. Pour in the hot Fish Fumet, stir until combined and spread out the ingredients evenly in the pan. Add the saffron and grate the zest of the limes over the paella, and bring to a boil. If you have a timer, set it to 17 minutes. Cook over high heat for 5 minutes until the rice rises to the surface of the liquid. Taste and season with salt, if necessary, bearing in mind that the flavours will become more pronounced as the liquid evaporates. Put the paella in the preheated oven for 9 minutes.

Remove the paella from the oven and arrange the king prawns, monkfish, squid, langoustines and mussels on top of the rice. Put the pan back in the oven for a further 3 minutes, then remove the paella once again. Cover the paella with a clean, damp dish towel, allow it to rest for 3 minutes, then serve.

ARROZ EN PAELLA DE RESTOS INTENCIONADOS DEL PUCHERO
PAELLA RICE WITH LEFT-OVERS

Serves 2
Preparation time: 35 minutes
Cooking time: 17 minutes

For the meatballs

50 g (⅓ cup) cooked boiling fowl, finely chopped

50 g (⅓ cup) cooked chicken, finely chopped

50 g (⅓ cup) cooked dry cured ham, finely chopped

50 g (⅓ cup) carrots (from the stew), finely chopped

50 g (½ cup) leeks (from the stew), finely chopped

2 tablespoons chopped flat-leaf parsley

25 g (½ cup) fresh breadcrumbs, soaked in milk and squeezed dry

1 egg, lightly beaten

25 g (¼ cup) plain (all-purpose) flour

100 ml (scant ½ cup) olive oil

For the paella rice

50 ml (¼ cup) Garlic Oil (page 60) or ordinary olive oil

25 g (¼ cup) cooked chickpeas

200 g (1 cup) bomba or other short-grain rice

100 g (⅓ cup) Tomato Sofrito (page 54) or passata (puréed canned tomatoes)

scant 1 teaspoon Spanish sweet smoked paprika

500 ml (2¼ cups) stock (from the stew)

1 cooking chorizo sausage (left over from the stew), cut into rounds

1 morcilla sausage (Spanish black pudding/blood sausage), left over from the stew, cut into rounds

¼ teaspoon saffron threads, toasted and pounded

salt

In Spain, left-overs are often used in paella. The following recipe calls for the left-overs of a stew (cocido or puchero, the latter a Spanish stew often made with chickpeas or beans), which can be made specially for this purpose. The stew left-overs can be eaten separately while the rice is cooking.

For a moist texture, use a 34-cm (13½-inch) paella pan suitable for use on the stove and in the oven. This paella can be served with Rocket (Arugula) Aioli (page 36).

To make the meatballs, put the chopped boiling fowl, chicken, ham, carrots and leeks into a medium mixing bowl. Add the parsley, breadcrumbs and egg. Mix well and shape the mixture into balls about 2 cm (1 inch) in diameter and coat with flour. Heat the olive oil in a frying pan or skillet over moderate heat, add the meatballs and sauté for about 10 minutes until lightly browned all over. Set aside.

Preheat the oven to 150°C/300°F/Gas Mark 2. Add the Garlic Oil to the paella pan set over low heat, add the chickpeas and gently sauté for a few minutes until lightly browned all over.

Add the rice and cook over low heat for a few minutes, stirring with a wooden spatula, until thoroughly coated and translucent; do not allow the rice to burn.

Add the Tomato Sofrito and stir well, deglazing the pan by scraping up any bits on the bottom of the pan with a wooden spatula. Add the paprika, stir through and cook over moderate heat for a few seconds, taking care that it does not burn. Pour in the stock and stir thoroughly, bring to a boil, then add the meatballs, chorizo and morcilla sausage, spreading them out evenly in the pan. Add the saffron. If you have a timer, set it to 17 minutes. Bring back to a boil and cook over very high heat for 5 minutes until the rice rises to the surface of the liquid. Taste the stock and season with salt, if necessary, bearing in mind that the flavours will become more pronounced as the liquid evaporates.

Put the paella in the preheated oven for 12 minutes. Remove it from the oven, allow it to rest for 2 minutes and serve.

ARROZ EN PAELLA CON JUDÍAS BLANCAS E ALBONDIGAS
PAELLA RICE WITH MEATBALLS AND HARICOT (NAVY) BEANS

Serves 2
Preparation time: 25 minutes
(excluding stock)
Cooking time: 17 minutes

For the meatballs

75 g (2½ oz) lean pork, finely chopped

75 g (2½ oz) beef, finely chopped

50 g (1¾ oz) onion, finely chopped

2 tablespoons chopped flat-leaf parsley

25 g (½ cup) fresh breadcrumbs, soaked in milk for 5 minutes and squeezed dry

1 egg, lightly beaten

25 g (¼ cup) all-purpose flour

100 ml (scant ½ cup) olive oil, to fry the meatballs

salt

For the paella rice

500 ml (2¼ cups) meat stock (ideally left over from a stew)

50 ml (¼ cup) Garlic Oil (page 60) or ordinary olive oil

100 g (2 cups) spring onions (scallions), diced

100 g (¾ cup) turnips, finely diced

whole hazelnuts

200 g (1 cup) bomba or other short-grain rice

50 g (⅓ cup) Tomato Sofrito (page 54) or passata (puréed canned tomatoes)

1 teaspoon Spanish sweet smoked paprika

150 g (¾ cup) cooked haricot (navy) beans

1 teaspoon saffron threads, toasted and pounded

1 celery stalk, strings removed, thinly sliced and set aside in a bowl of iced water

salt

For a moist texture, use a 34-cm (13½-inch) paella pan suitable for use on the stove and in the oven.

To make the meatballs, put the finely chopped meats and onion into a medium mixing bowl. Add the parsley, breadcrumbs and egg. Season with salt, mix these ingredients well and shape the mixture into meatballs 2 cm (1 inch) in diameter. Allow 4 or 5 meatballs per person. Coat the meatballs with flour. Pour the olive oil into a frying pan or skillet set over moderate heat, add the meatballs and sauté for about 10 minutes until browned all over. Take out of the pan and set aside.

In a separate saucepan, heat the stock without allowing it to boil. Preheat the oven to 150°C/300°F/Gas Mark 2.

Heat the Garlic Oil in the paella pan set over low heat, add the spring onions (scallions), turnips and hazelnuts and gently sauté for a few minutes until the vegetables have softened.

Add the rice and cook over low heat for a few minutes, stirring with a wooden spatula, until thoroughly coated and translucent; do not allow the rice to burn. Add the Tomato Sofrito and stir well, deglazing the pan by scraping up any bits on the bottom of the pan with a wooden spatula. Allow to cook until the mixture has reduced and thickened.

Add the paprika, stir through and cook over moderate heat for a few seconds, taking care that it does not burn. Add the very hot stock and the haricot beans, bring to a boil, then arrange the meatballs evenly over the rice. Add the saffron. If you have a timer, set it to 17 minutes. Cook over very high heat for 5 minutes until the rice rises to the surface of the liquid. Taste and season with salt, if necessary, bearing in mind that the flavours will become more pronounced as the liquid evaporates. Put the paella in the preheated oven for 12 minutes.

Remove the paella from the oven and allow it to rest for 3 minutes. Meanwhile, drain the celery strips and blot them dry with paper towels. Sprinkle the celery over the top of the rice and serve.

PAELLA RICE WITH MARINATED SPARE RIBS

Serves 2
Preparation time:
30 minutes (excluding stock) +
12 hours marinating
Cooking time: 17 minutes

For the spare rib marinade

1 teaspoon Spanish sweet
smoked paprika

1 teaspoon ground caraway seeds

1 teaspoon ground cumin

1 teaspoon ground coriander

1 teaspoon ground white peppercorns

1 clove garlic, finely chopped

2 tablespoons grated fresh ginger

1 teaspoon salt

1 teaspoon dried oregano

100 ml (scant ½ cup) olive oil

6 spare ribs (ready to use, cut into
single ribs)

For the paella rice

400 ml (1¾ cups) Ibérico Ham Stock
(page 50)

50 ml (¼ cup) Garlic Oil (page 60) or
ordinary olive oil

2 onions, finely chopped

200 g (1 cup) bomba or other short-
grain rice

50 ml (¼ cup) sherry vinegar

1 tablespoon honey

100 g (⅓ cup) Tomato Sofrito (page 54)
or passata (puréed canned tomatoes)

½ teaspoon Spanish sweet
smoked paprika

¼ teaspoon saffron threads, toasted
and pounded

1 tablespoon raisins, soaked in cold
water to rehydrate

salt

For a moist texture, use a 34-cm (13½-inch) paella pan suitable for use on the stove and in the oven.

The day before you plan to serve this dish, make the marinade for the pork by mixing all the spices, herbs and the olive oil together. Marinate the spare ribs in the marinade for 12 hours in the refrigerator. The following day, place spare ribs on a rack to drain. Heat the Ibérico Ham Stock without allowing it to boil. Preheat the oven to 150°C/300°F/Gas Mark 2.

Heat the Garlic Oil in a paella pan over low heat. Add the drained spare ribs and sauté for several minutes until browned all over. Add the chopped onion and gently sauté for a few minutes until translucent but not browned.

Add the rice and and cook over low heat for a few minutes, stirring with a wooden spatula, until thoroughly coated and translucent; do not allow the rice to burn. Add the vinegar and honey and mix well, then pour in the Tomato Sofrito and mix well. Deglaze the pan by scraping up any bits on the bottom of the pan with a wooden spatula. Allow the mixture to cook until it has reduced and thickened.

Add the paprika, stir through and cook over moderate heat for a few seconds, taking care that it does not burn. Pour in the hot ham stock, stir and bring to a boil over very high heat. Add the saffron and the raisins. If you have a timer, set it to 17 minutes. Continue to cook over very high heat for 5 minutes until the rice rises to the surface of the liquid. Taste and season with salt, if necessary, bearing in mind that the flavours will become more pronounced as the liquid evaporates. Arrange the spare ribs on top of the rice and put the paella in the preheated oven for 12 minutes.

Remove the paella from the oven, allow it to rest for 3 minutes, then serve.

PAELLA RICE WITH SPRING VEGETABLES

Serves 2
Preparation time: 25 minutes
(excluding stock)
Cooking time: 17 minutes

600 ml (2½ cups) Vegetable Stock
(page 38)

50 g (⅓ cup) broad (fava) beans,
shelled

2 small, tender very fresh tender
baby artichokes

1 lemon, quartered

50 ml (¼ cup) olive oil

2 small new carrots

4 small young turnips

200 g (7 oz) spring onions (scallions),
cut into fine strips

½ bunch green asparagus, woody
stems removed

150 g (1 cup) fresh peas, shelled

1 clove garlic, finely chopped

200 g (1 cup) bomba or other short-
grain rice

200 g (⅔ cup) Tomato Sofrito (page 54)
or passata (puréed canned tomatoes)

½ teaspoon Spanish sweet
smoked paprika

¼ teaspoon saffron threads, toasted
and pounded

salt and pepper

The vegetables for this paella can vary according to the seasons: in winter, for example, choose tubers and root vegetables, such as parsnips, celeriac (celery root), carrots, turnips, Hamburg parsley roots and Jerusalem artichokes.

For a moist texture, use a 34-cm (13½-inch) paella pan suitable for use on the stove and in the oven.

Heat the Vegetable Stock without allowing it to boil. Preheat the oven to 150°C/300°F/Gas Mark 2.

Blanch the broad (fava) beans in boiling water for 5 seconds, then rinse them immediately under cold running water. Remove their outer skins. Wash and trim the artichokes, rub the cut surfaces with lemon juice to prevent discoloration and set aside in a bowl of cold water acidulated with lemon juice.

Heat the olive oil in the paella pan over moderate heat, add all the vegetables and sauté for 2 minutes until they begin to brown. Add the garlic in the centre of the pan and sauté for several minutes until the vegetables have softened.

Add the rice and cook over low heat for a few minutes, stirring with a wooden spatula, until thoroughly coated and translucent; do not allow the rice to burn. Pour in the Tomato Sofrito and stir well, deglazing the pan by scraping up any bits on the bottom of the pan with a wooden spatula.

Add the paprika, stir through and cook over moderate heat for a few seconds, taking care that it does not burn. Pour in the hot stock, stir and bring to a boil. Add the saffron. If you have a timer, set it to 17 minutes. Continue to cook over moderate heat for 5 minutes until the rice rises to the surface of the liquid. Taste the stock and season with salt, if necessary, bearing in mind that the flavours will be more pronounced as the liquid evaporates. Put the paella in the preheated oven for 12 minutes.

Remove the paella from the oven, allow it to rest for 3 minutes, then serve.

ARROZ EN PAELLA DE TRUFA NEGRA EN COSTRA
PAELLA RICE WITH EGGS AND BLACK TRUFFLE

Serves 2
Chilling time for eggs, rice and truffles: 3 or 4 days
Soaking time for the chickpeas: 12 hours
Preparation time of the stock and meat: about 6 hours (make this in advance)
Preparation time: 30 minutes (excluding stock)
Cooking time: 17 minutes

6 fresh eggs

1 black truffle, about 50 g (2 oz)

For the stock

50 g (¼ cup) chickpeas

1 pig's trotter (foot)

1 pig's ear, thoroughly cleaned

1 pig's tongue

300 g (11 oz) bones from a ham

2 bay leaves

2 cloves garlic

3 black peppercorns

For the paella rice

50 ml (¼ cup) Garlic Oil (page 60) or ordinary olive oil

150 g (5 oz) fresh Ibérico pork (shoulder section of loin), diced

50 g (⅓ cup) turnips, diced

1 onion, diced

3 cloves garlic, finely chopped

1 dried ñora pepper, stalk and seeds removed, finely crumbled

200 g (1 cup) bomba or other short-grain rice

100 g (⅓ cup) Tomato Sofrito (page 54) or passata (puréed canned tomatoes)

½ teaspoon Spanish sweet smoked paprika

¼ teaspoon saffron threads, toasted and pounded

salt, plus coarse salt for the meats

This paella is usually made in an earthenware dish. For a moist texture, use a 34-cm (13½-inch) paella pan suitable for use on the stove and in the oven.

Three or four days before you begin, wash and dry the eggs and truffle. Put them on top of the rice in an airtight container (it is important that the eggs and truffle be in direct contact with the rice). Seal the container hermetically and store in the refrigerator. The rice and eggs will take on the flavour of the truffle. The day before you plan to serve the dish, soak the chickpeas in cold water.

About 6 hours in advance, or the day before, sprinkle coarse salt all over the meats, allow to rest for 1 hour, then soak in cold water for 15 minutes to remove excess salt. Pour 3 litres (13¼ cups) water into a large pan over high heat and add the pig's trotter (foot), ear, tongue, bones, bay leaf, garlic and peppercorns. Bring to a boil and add the chickpeas. Reduce the heat and cook for about 2 hours, skimming off the fat as the meat cooks. When all the meats are tender, remove them and the chickpeas from of the pan. Strain the cooking liquid to use for cooking the rice. Measure 600 ml (2¼ cups) stock and keep it hot.

Skin and trim the tongue, clean and cut it into dice. Bone the trotter and lay it flat. Stuff it with the diced tongue and roll it up tightly to form a 3-cm (1-inch) roll. Tie it up tightly with kitchen string and chill in the refrigerator. Cut the pig's ear into 2-cm (1-inch) dice. Cut the stuffed trotter into 2-cm (1-inch) slices. Heat the stock but do not allow it to boil. Preheat the oven to 150°C/300°F/Gas Mark 2.

Heat the Garlic Oil in the pan over very low heat, add the diced pork and sauté for a few minutes until browned all over. Set aside, covered with aluminium foil. Add the turnips, onion, garlic and ñora pepper to the pan and sauté until lightly browned and softened. Add the rice and cook over low heat for a few minutes, stirring, until thoroughly coated and translucent; do not allow it to burn. Add the Tomato Sofrito and stir well. When it is well incorporated into the rest of the ingredients, add the paprika and cook for a few seconds, taking care that it does not burn. Add the hot stock, stir and bring to a boil. Add the pig's ear, chickpeas, tongue and trotter slices, then add the saffron and cook over moderate heat for 5 minutes until the rice rises to the surface of the liquid. Taste the stock and season with salt, if necessary, bearing in mind that the flavours will become more pronounced as the liquid evaporates. Put the paella in the preheated oven for 9 minutes.

While it is cooking, beat the truffle-flavoured eggs. Remove the paella from the oven and pour the beaten eggs over the rice. They should cover the rice completely. Return the paella to the oven for a further 3 minutes. Remove the pan from the oven and allow the paella to rest for 3 minutes. Meanwhile, slice the truffle into very fine shavings. Arrange these evenly on top of the rice and serve.

ARROZ EN PAELLA MÁS QUE NEGRO
'ULTRA-BLACK' PAELLA RICE

Serves 2
Preparation time: 25 minutes
(excluding fumet)
Cooking time: 17 minutes

400 ml (1¾ cups) Fish Fumet (page 48)

100 ml (scant ½ cup) olive oil

2 cloves garlic, finely chopped

200 g (7 oz) horn-of-plenty (black chanterelle) mushrooms, cleaned

200 g (7 oz) cuttlefish, white part only, washed and cut into 1-cm (½-inch) dice

200 g (1 cup) bomba or other short-grain rice

200 g (⅔ cup) Tomato Sofrito (page 54) or passata (puréed canned tomatoes)

2 sachets cuttlefish ink, about 40 g (1½ oz), available from Spanish or Italian grocery shops

½ teaspoon Spanish sweet smoked paprika

salt

This recipe was inspired by Pierre Soulages, the French artist who created the concept of outre-noir ('ultra-black'), a novel way of looking at this 'colour' and 'an invitation to see the light beyond black'. This paella is a culinary expression of his artistic theories. For a moist texture, use a 34-cm (13½-inch) paella pan suitable for use on the stove and in the oven.

Heat the Fish Fumet but do not allow it to boil. Preheat the oven to 150°C/300°F/Gas Mark 2.

Heat the oil in the paella pan over low heat, add the garlic and, once it is golden, add the horn-of-plenty mushrooms. Gently sauté for several minutes until all the liquid from the mushrooms has evaporated. Add the diced cuttlefish and cook for several minutes until the liquid from the cuttlefish has evaporated. Push the squid and mushrooms towards the edge of the pan.

Add the rice to the centre of the pan and cook over low heat for a few minutes, stirring with a wooden spatula, until thoroughly coated and translucent; do not allow the rice to burn. Add the Tomato Sofrito and the cuttlefish ink and stir well, deglazing the pan by scraping up any bits on the bottom of the pan with a wooden spatula.

Add the paprika, stir through and cook over moderate heat for a few seconds, taking care that it does not burn. Pour in the very hot Fish Fumet. Spread the rice out evenly to cover the bottom of the paella pan completely. Bring to a boil. If you have a timer, set it to 17 minutes. Cook over high heat for 5 minutes, until the rice rises to the surface of the liquid. Taste the fumet and season with salt, bearing in mind that the flavours will become more pronounced as the liquid evaporates.

Spread the rice out again in the pan and put the paella in the preheated oven for 12 minutes. Remove the paella from the oven, allow it to rest for 3 minutes, then serve.

WHITE PAELLA RICE WITH SOLE AND CHAMPAGNE

Serves 2
Preparation time: 35 minutes
(excluding fumet)
Cooking time: 17 minutes

200 g (1⅓ cups) fresh broad (fava) beans, shelled

1 bunch French tarragon, leaves only

oil for frying

500 ml (2¼ cups) Fish Fumet (page 48)

100 ml (scant ½ cup) Citrus-flavoured Oil (page 60) or ordinary olive oil

1 large sole, 40 cm (16 inches) in length, filleted by the fish supplier (ask for the bones and head in one piece), the bones washed and dried, the fillets cut into 30-g (1¼-oz) pieces

150 g (2⅔ cups) spring onions (scallions), finely sliced

200 g (1 cup) bomba or other short-grain rice

200 ml (scant 1 cup) Champagne

1 teaspoon Lemon Relish (page 57)

½ teaspoon Spanish sweet smoked paprika

100 g (3½ oz) fresh white asparagus tips

salt

The sole bones play an integral role in this recipe because the natural gelatine they contain seeps into the rice, and this gives the dish a different result from that which would be obtained from using the bones to make a fumet. For an extra-fine texture, use a 41-cm (16-inch) paella pan suitable for use on the stove and in the oven.

Plunge the broad (fava) beans in boiling water, bring back to a boil, take them out and immerse immediately in iced water. Remove the outer skin of the broad beans and set them aside. Heat about 2 cm (¾ inch) of the oil for frying in a heavy-base pan and fry the tarragon leaves in oil until crisp. Set aside on paper towels. Heat the Fish Fumet but do not allow it to boil. Preheat the oven to 180°C/350°F/Gas Mark 4.

Heat the Citrus-flavoured Oil in the paella pan over low heat. Add the spring onions (scallions) to the pan and gently sauté for a few minutes; do not allow them to colour.

Add the rice and cook over low heat for a few minutes, stirring with a wooden spatula, until thoroughly coated and translucent; do not allow the rice to burn. Pour in the Champagne, stir vigorously and deglaze the pan by scraping up any bits on the bottom of the pan with a wooden spatula.

Add the Lemon Relish and paprika, stir through and cook over moderate heat for a few seconds without allowing the mixture to burn. Pour in the hot fumet and spread the rice out evenly over the paella pan. Bring to a boil. Taste and season with salt, if necessary, bearing in mind that the flavours will become more concentrated as the liquid evaporates. Add the broad (fava) beans and asparagus tips. If you have a timer, set it to 17 minutes and cook over very high heat. After 4 minutes, place the sole's carcass on top of the rice and liquid with the head nearest you and the tail furthest away, and cook for a further 2 minutes.

Check the position of the carcass laid flat on top of the rice and put the paella in the preheated oven for 8 minutes. Remove the paella from the oven, add the sole fillets to their place in the sole carcass and return to the oven for a further 3 minutes.

Remove the paella from the oven. Allow it to rest for 2 minutes, sprinkle the fried tarragon leaves over the rice and serve.

Serves 2
Preparation time: 25 minutes
(excluding stock)
Cooking time: 17 minutes

50 ml (¼ cup) olive oil

1 ñora pepper, stalk and seeds
removed, coarsely crumbled

1 clove garlic, finely chopped

500 ml (2¼ cups) Pork Stock (page 50)

1 boned ham hock, cut into 50-g (2-oz)
pieces

50 ml (¼ cup) Garlic Oil (page 60) or
ordinary olive oil

2×1-cm (½-inch) slices Morteau
sausage

×1-cm (½-inch) slices garlic sausage

70 g (⅔ cup) Savoy cabbage, chopped

100 g (3½ oz) cooked salt pork belly
(side), diced

150 g (¾ cup) bomba or other short-
grain rice

100 ml (scant ½ cup) beer (such as San
Miguel or other light beer)

00 g (13 cup) Tomato Sofrito (page 54)
or passata (puréed canned tomatoes)

teaspoon Spanish sweet
smoked paprika

teaspoon saffron, toasted and
pounded

50 g (¾ cup) cooked brown lentils

salt

For a moist texture, use a 34-cm (13½-inch) paella pan suitable for use on the stove and in the oven.

Heat the olive oil in a saucepan over low heat, add the ñora pepper and garlic, and gently sauté for a few minutes until the garlic is golden. Remove the ingredients from the pan, put them into a mortar and pound to a paste with the pestle. Set aside. Heat the Pork Stock but do not allow it to boil. Preheat the oven to 150°C/300°F/Gas Mark 2.

Pour the Garlic Oil into the paella pan over low heat, add the sausage slices and ham hock and sauté for a few minutes until lightly browned. Add the cabbage and then the pork belly (side) to the pan and sauté over moderate heat for a few minutes until lightly browned all over, then add the pounded garlic and ñora pepper paste.

Add the rice and cook over low heat for a few minutes, stirring with a wooden spatula, until thoroughly coated and translucent; do not allow the rice to burn. Pour in the beer and mix all the ingredients well, deglazing the pan by scraping up any bits on the bottom of the pan with a wooden spatula. Add the Tomato Sofrito and mix all the ingredients thoroughly.

Add the paprika, stir through and cook over moderate heat for a few seconds, taking care that it does not burn. Pour in the hot stock, stir and bring to a boil. If you have a timer, set it to 17 minutes. Add the saffron and continue to cook over very high heat for 5 minutes, until the rice rises to the surface of the liquid. Taste and season with salt if necessary, bearing in mind that the flavours will be more concentrated as the liquid evaporates. Mix the lentils into the rice.

Put the paella in the preheated oven for 12 minutes. Remove the paella from the oven, allow it to rest for 3 minutes, then serve.

PAELLA RICE 'A BANDA' WITH TURBOT

Serves 2
Preparation time: 25 minutes
(excluding fumet)
Cooking time: 17 minutes

bones from 1 turbot, about 30 cm
(12 inches) in length, including the
backbone and head, not including the
fillets or gills

500 ml (1¼ cups) Fish Fumet (page 48)
made with some of the turbot fillets
(not with the bones)

50 ml (¼ cup) Citrus-flavoured Oil
(page 60) or ordinary olive oil

2 large spring onions (scallions), white
parts chopped and green parts sliced

2 Japanese or Chinese spring onions
(scallions), white parts chopped and
green parts sliced into rounds

100 ml (scant ½ cup) mirin

100 ml (scant ½ cup) rice wine vinegar

200 g (1 cup) bomba or other short-
grain rice

1 teaspoon Spanish sweet
smoked paprika

8 g (¼ oz) iriko dashi (Japanese stock
powder)

zest of 1 lime, finely grated

25 g (1 cup) large spinach stalks
(without the leaves), snipped

salt

*For this recipe you will only need the bones of the turbot and its
head. The fillets, or rather some of the fillets (for turbot is a large
fish), will be used to make the fumet, and can be eaten with the
rice. The spinach leaves will also be used for the fumet: only their
stalks are used as a garnish. Mirin, Japanese spring onions and
iriko dashi are available in Asian grocery shops.*

*For an extra-fine texture, use a 41-cm (16-inch) paella pan
suitable for use on the stove and in the oven.*

Soak the turbot bones in very cold water for 30 minutes to get rid
of any remaining blood. Drain and pat completely dry with paper
towels. Heat the Fish Fumet made with the turbot but do not
allow it to boil. Preheat the oven to 180°C/350°F/Gas Mark 4.

Heat the oil in the paella pan over low heat, add the chopped
spring onion (scallion) bulbs and gently sauté for a few minutes
without allowing them to brown. Add the mirin and the vinegar,
stir briskly and deglaze the pan by scraping up the bits on the bottom of the pan with a wooden spatula. Continue to cook to reduce
the mixture until there is virtually no moisture remaining.

Add the rice and cook over low heat for a few minutes, stirring
with a wooden spatula, until thoroughly coated and translucent; do
not allow the rice to burn.

Add the paprika, stir through and cook over moderate heat for
a few seconds, taking care that it does not burn. Pour in the hot
fumet and spread the rice out evenly in the pan. Add the iriko
dashi. Taste the mixture and season with salt, if necessary, bearing in mind that the flavours will become more pronounced as the
liquid evaporates. Sprinkle the surface with finely grated lime
zest. If you have a timer, set it to 17 minutes, and continue to cook
over high heat.

After 4 minutes, add the turbot skeleton to the pan, laying it flat
and at right angles to the pan's handles, with head and tail just
touching the pan's back and front edges. Cook for 2 minutes, then
press the turbot bones into the rice – the boiling fumet may have
dislodged it. Put the paella in the preheated oven for 11 minutes.

Remove the paella from the oven. Sprinkle it with the spring
onion rounds and spinach stalks, then allow it to rest for 2 minutes.
Place a section of the turbot's skeleton on each person's plate with
the rice.

PAELLA RICE WITH SARDINES AND OLIVES

Serves 2
Preparation time: 40 minutes
(excluding fumet)
Cooking time: 17 minutes + 30 minutes
for the sardine-flavoured oil

300 ml (1¼ cups) olive oil

900 g (2 lb) whole fresh sardines, filleted, reserving the livers and trimmings (bones, heads and guts)

600 ml (2½ cups) Fish Fumet (page 48)

200 g (7 oz) spring onions (scallions), sliced into thin strips

¼ fennel bulb, sliced into thin strips

60 g (½ cup) stoned (pitted) black olives, preferably Fogón-style Olives (page 57)

1 clove garlic, finely chopped

200 g (1 cup) bomba or other short-grain rice

200 g (⅔ cup) Tomato Sofrito (page 54) or passata (puréed canned tomatoes)

½ teaspoon Spanish sweet smoked paprika

¼ teaspoon saffron threads, toasted and pounded

salt and pepper

If you like, you can serve half a fennel bulb, very finely sliced (use a mandolin) and dressed in a vinaigrette at the last minute, to accompany this paella. Just before serving, place the dressed fennel slices in the centre.

For an extra-fine texture, use a 41-cm (16-inch) paella pan suitable for use on the stove and in the oven.

To make sardine-flavoured oil, heat the olive oil over very low heat, add half the sardine trimmings and cook very gently for about 30 minutes, until the trimmings become dry and crisp. Strain the oil and set it aside.

In a saucepan set over high heat, add the fumet and the remaining sardine trimmings and heat until it reaches boiling point, then reduce the heat to very low and leave to simmer very gently for 15 minutes. Strain and keep hot. Preheat the oven to 150°C/300°F/Gas Mark 2.

Heat the sardine-flavoured oil in the paella pan over low heat, add the spring onions (scallions), fennel and olives and sauté for a few minutes before adding the garlic. Continue to sauté for a few minutes more until all the ingredients are lightly brown.

Add the rice and cook over low heat for a few minutes, stirring with a wooden spatula, until thoroughly coated and translucent; do not allow the rice to burn. Add the sardine livers and stir, then add the Tomato Sofrito and mix all the ingredients thoroughly, deglazing the pan by scraping up any bits on the bottom of the pan with a wooden spatula. Allow to cook until the mixture has reduced and thickened.

Add the paprika, stir through and cook over moderate heat for a few seconds, taking care it does not burn. Pour in the very hot fumet, stir and bring to a boil. Add the saffron. If you have a timer, set it to 17 minutes. Cook over very high heat for 5 minutes, until the rice rises to the surface of the liquid. Taste and season with salt, if necessary, bearing in mind that the flavours will become more pronounced as the liquid evaporates.

Put the paella in the preheated oven for 9 minutes. Remove the paella from the oven and quickly arrange the sardine fillets on the surface. Return the paella pan to the oven for a further 3 minutes. Remove the paella from the oven once again, allow it to rest for 3 minutes, then serve.

PAELLA RICE WITH SOFT-SHELL CRABS

Serves 2
Preparation time: 25 minutes
(excluding fumet)
Cooking time: 17 minutes

1 small bunch tarragon, leaves only

3 tablespoons olive oil, plus extra
for frying

600 ml (2½ cups) Shellfish Fumet
(page 47)

6 frozen soft-shell crabs, thawed

2 whole baby carrots

2 whole baby turnips

½ bunch green asparagus, woody
ends removed, tips reserved whole,
and tender stems cut into thin strips

200 g (7 oz) spring onions (scallions),
cut into thin strips

50 g (⅓ cup) broad (fava) beans,
shelled, blanched and outer
skins removed

50 g (⅓ cup) peas, shelled
and blanched

1 clove garlic, finely chopped

200 g (1 cup) bomba or other short-
grain rice

200 g (⅔ cup) Tomato Sofrito (page 54)
or passata (puréed canned tomatoes)

½ teaspoon Spanish sweet
smoked paprika

¼ teaspoon saffron threads, toasted
and pounded

salt

For a moist texture, use a 34-cm (13½-inch) paella pan suitable for use on the stove and in the oven.

Heat 2 cm (¾ inch) olive oil in a heavy-base pan and fry the tarragon leaves in oil until they are crisp. Set them aside to drain on paper towels. Heat the Shellfish Fumet but do not allow it to boil. Preheat the oven to 150°C/300°F/Gas Mark 2.

Heat the olive oil in the paella pan set over moderate heat, add the soft-shell crabs and sauté for 2 minutes until browned, then push them to the side of the pan. Add the vegetables and garlic to the centre of the pan and sauté for several minutes until they are very lightly browned.

Add the rice and cook over low heat for a few minutes, stirring with a wooden spatula, until thoroughly coated and translucent; do not allow the rice to burn. Add the Tomato Sofrito and stir well, deglazing the pan by scraping up any bits on the bottom of the pan with a wooden spatula. Allow to cook until the mixture has reduced and thickened.

Add the paprika, stir through and cook over moderate heat for a few seconds, taking care that it does not burn. Pour in the hot fumet, stir and bring to boil. Add the saffron. If you have a timer, set it to 17 minutes. Cook over very high heat for 5 minutes until the rice rises to the surface of the liquid. Taste and season with salt, if necessary, bearing in mind that the flavours will become more pronounced as the liquid evaporates.

Arrange the crabs on top of the rice. Put the paella in the pre-heated oven for 12 minutes. Remove the paella from the oven and allow it to rest for 3 minutes. Garnish with the fried tarragon and serve.

ARROZ EN PAELLA BLANCA CON ANGUILA
WHITE PAELLA RICE WITH EEL

Serves 2
Preparation time: 40 minutes
(excluding stock)
Cooking time: 17 minutes

400 g (14 oz) eels, with the skin on, cleaned and cut into sections, each weighing 50 g (2 oz)

300 ml (1¼ cups) Japanese eel sauce (unagi kabayaki no tare)

500 ml (2¼ cups) Eel Stock (page 40)

100 ml (scant ½ cup) Ginger Oil (page 60) or ordinary olive oil

1 clove garlic

2 onions, finely chopped

200 g (1 cup) bomba or other short-grain rice

½ teaspoon Spanish sweet smoked paprika

200 g (7 oz) white radish or mooli (daikon), cut into thin sticks

3 tablespoons sesame oil

2 teaspoons rice vinegar

20 g (¾ oz) bottarga (cured grey mullet roe), grated

salt

For an extra-fine texture, use a 41-cm (16-inch) paella pan suitable for use on the stove and in the oven.

Use the grill (broiler), or a salamander if you have one, to grill (broil) the pieces of eel, basting and turning them at frequent intervals with 200 ml (scant 1 cup) Japanese eel sauce, until their surfaces are caramelized all over. Set them aside. Heat the Eel Stock but do not allow it to boil. Preheat the oven to 150°C/300°F/Gas Mark 2.

Heat the Ginger Oil in the paella pan over moderate heat, add the whole garlic clove and the chopped onions and sauté for about 5 minutes until the onions are very soft.

Add the rice and cook over low heat for a few minutes, stirring with a wooden spatula, until thoroughly coated and translucent; do not allow the rice to burn. Add 100 ml (scant ½ cup) Japanese eel sauce and stir well, deglazing the pan by scraping up any bits on the bottom of the pan with a wooden spatula.

Add the paprika, stir through and cook over moderate heat for a few seconds, taking care that it does not burn. Remove and discard the garlic clove. Pour in the hot fumet and spread the rice out evenly in the paella pan. If you have a timer, set it to 17 minutes. Taste and season with salt, if necessary, bearing in mind that the flavours will become more pronounced as the liquid evaporates. Bring to a boil and cook over very high heat for 5 minutes, until the rice rises to the surface of the liquid.

Spread the rice out again in an even layer covering the bottom of the paella pan, then place the pieces of eel in the pan. Put the paella in the preheated oven for 12 minutes. Meanwhile, make a dressing by combining the sesame oil and the rice vinegar, and use it to dress the white radish.

Remove the paella from the oven and allow it to rest for 3 minutes. Sprinkle the grated bottarga over the surface of the paella and serve, with the dressed white radish served separately in a bowl.

PAELLA RICE WITH LOBSTER, BABY CUTTLEFISH AND FENNEL

Serves 2
Preparation time: 25 minutes
Cooking time: 17 minutes

1 live flat slipper lobster,
spiny (rock) lobster or ordinary lobster,
about 800 g (1¾ lb)

50 ml (¼ cup) olive oil

1 dried ñora pepper, stalk removed and
seeded, coarsely crumbled

1 clove garlic

1 bitter almond

100 ml (scant ½ cup) Garlic Oil (see
page 60) or ordinary olive oil

100 g (3½ oz) baby cuttlefish, cleaned
and washed

150 g (1⅓ cups) fennel bulb, cut into
small dice

200 g (1 cup) bomba or other short-
grain rice

200 g (⅔ cup) Tomato Sofrito (page 54)
or passata (puréed canned tomatoes)

½ teaspoon Spanish sweet
smoked paprika

¼ teaspoon saffron threads, toasted
and pounded

salt

*For an extra-fine texture, use a 41-cm (16-inch) paella pan
suitable for use on the stove and in the oven.*

Preheat the oven to 150°C/300°F/Gas Mark 2. Hold the lobster,
right side up, on a chopping (cutting) board and, using a large,
very sharp kitchen knife, cut the lobster's head away from its
body. Cut lengthwise down the exact centre of the lobster's tail,
slicing it in half, leaving the legs attached. Reserve all the liquid
released from the lobster.

Heat the olive oil in the paella pan over low heat. Add the ñora
pepper, the whole garlic clove and the bitter almond and sauté
for a few minutes until the garlic clove is lightly browned. Remove
the ingredients from the pan, put into a mortar and pound
together with a pestle. Set aside. Heat 600 ml (2½ cups) water.

Heat the Garlic Oil in the paella pan over low heat, then add the
baby cuttlefish, fennel and all the lobster parts, flesh side downwards. Season with salt and sauté gently for a few minutes until
the lobster has browned all over. Remove the mixture from the
pan and set aside in a deep dish, covered with aluminium foil.

Add the reserved liquid released by the lobster and the cuttlefish
to the pan and heat until it has evaporated. Add the rice and cook
over low heat for a few minutes, stirring with a wooden spatula,
until thoroughly coated and translucent; do not allow the rice
to burn. Add the Tomato Sofrito and stir all the ingredients well,
deglazing the pan by scraping up any bits on the bottom of the pan
with a wooden spatula.

Add the paprika, stir through and cook over moderate heat for
a few seconds, taking care that it does not burn. Pour in the hot
water. Add the ñora pepper, garlic and bitter almond paste.
Bring to a boil. If you have a timer, set it to 17 minutes. Add the
saffron and allow to cook over high heat for 5 minutes until the
rice rises to the surface of the liquid. Taste and season with salt,
if necessary, bearing in mind that the flavours will become more
pronounced as the liquid evaporates.

Place the lobster, cut sides downwards, on top of the paella. Put
the paella in the preheated oven for 12 minutes. Remove it from
the oven, allow it to rest for 3 minutes, then serve.

PAELLA RICE WITH LOBSTER

Serves 2
Preparation time: 30 minutes
Cooking time: 17 minutes

1 live lobster, about 800 g (1¾ lb)

1 tablespoon olive oil

200 g (7 oz) tomatoes, halved, seeded and grated, skin discarded

100 ml (scant ½ cup) Lobster Oil (see page 62), Garlic Oil (see page 60) or ordinary olive oil

1 squid, about 60 g (2 oz), cleaned and cut into small dice

200 g (1 cup) bomba or other short-grain rice

½ teaspoon Spanish sweet smoked paprika

¼ teaspoon saffron threads, toasted and pounded

salt

For a moist texture, use a 34-cm (13½-inch) paella pan suitable for use on the stove and in the oven.

Preheat the oven to 150°C/300°F/Gas Mark 2. Heat the olive oil in a pan and fry the tomatoes for a few minutes, then set aside.

Use a heavy, very sharp kitchen knife to cut the lobster lengthwise in half. To do this, hold the lobster, legs downwards, on the surface. Push the tip of the knife into the head between the eyes and then lower the knife blade on to the centre of the rounded back, bringing it down gently but firmly so that the blade cuts through the entire head, body and tail, cutting it into two equal halves. Remove the black intestinal tract and the leathery, gritty stomach from the head. Collect all the liquid from the shell. Crack open the pincers without detaching them from the body. Set aside. Heat 600 ml (2½ cups) water.

Heat the Lobster Oil in the paella pan over low heat. Add the squid and the two halves of the lobster, flesh downwards. Add a little salt and sauté for a few minutes until lightly browned. When the lobster starts to change colour, turn it over and cook until it has turned red. Take it out of the pan and place in a dish, covered with aluminium foil.

Continue to cook the liquids from the lobster and the squid for several minutes until they evaporate. Add the rice and cook over low heat for a few minutes, stirring with a wooden spatula, until thoroughly coated and translucent; do not allow the rice to burn. Add the fried tomato and stir well, deglazing the pan by scraping up any bits on the bottom of the pan with a wooden spatula.

Add the paprika, stir through and cook over moderate heat for a few seconds, taking care that it does not burn. Pour in the hot water and bring to a fast boil over high heat. If you have a timer, set it to 17 minutes. Add the saffron. After 5 minutes, the rice will rise to the surface of the liquid. Taste and season with salt, if necessary, bearing in mind that the flavours will become more pronounced as the liquid evaporates.

Arrange the lobster on top of the rice, shell side uppermost. Put the paella in the preheated oven for 12 minutes. Remove the paella from the oven. Allow it to rest for 3 minutes, then serve.

PAELLA RICE WITH LANGOUSTINES AND MOREL MUSHROOMS

Serves 2
Preparation time: 1 hour (including fumet and sofrito)
Cooking time: 17 minutes

6 languoustines, about 80 g (2¾ oz) each

50 g (2 oz) fresh morel mushrooms, carefully cleaned and rinsed

trimmings and tentacles of squid for the rice

For the langoustine and mushroom sofrito

100 ml (scant ½ cup) Langoustine Oil (see page 62) or ordinary olive oil

1 ñora pepper, stalk and seeds removed, coarsely crumbled

3 cloves garlic

langoustine heads, reserved from the langoustines for the fumet

½ green bell pepper, seeded, peeled and cut into fine strips

100 g (3½ oz) spring onions (scallions), cut into fine strips

1 shallot, finely sliced

50 g (2 oz) fresh morel mushrooms, carefully cleaned and rinsed, cut into fine strips

1 ripe tomato, peeled, seeded and grated, skin discarded

For the paella rice

100 ml (scant ½ cup) Langoustine Oil (page 62) or ordinary olive oil

1 squid, about 60 g (2 oz), cleaned and cut into small dice (keep the trimmings and tentacles for making the fumet)

200 g (1 cup) bomba or other short-grain rice

½ teaspoon Spanish sweet smoked paprika

¼ teaspoon saffron, toasted and pounded

200 g (7 oz) fresh best-quality morel mushrooms, carefully cleaned and rinsed, halved if large

zest of 1 lime

salt

I have chosen to prepare the sofrito separately for this recipe. This is a different technique, perhaps a more professional one and very common in Catalonia. Sofritos prepared in this way vary from recipe to recipe and can be enhanced by various flavourings. Reserve the best morels for the paella, using the poorest quality ones for the fumet. Use a 34-cm (13½-inch) paella pan suitable for use on the stove and in the oven.

To make the fumet, rinse the langoustines, then detach their heads and claws. Set the heads aside. Crush the claws in a mortar using a pestle and make a fumet with the crushed claws, the heads, the morels and the squid trimmings and tentacles (follow the Langoustine and Mushroom Fumet recipe on page 46). Working from the tail towards the head, shell uppermost, slice the langoustine tails lengthwise, leaving them attached to the head and stopping short of completely separating the two halves. Remove the black intestinal tract and press the two halves back together. Set aside.

To make the sofrito, heat the Langoustine Oil in a pan over low heat, add the ñora pepper and garlic cloves and sauté for a few minutes until the garlic is lightly browned. Add the reserved langoustine heads, green bell pepper, spring onions (scallions), shallot and morel mushrooms and sauté until the vegetables have cooked through. Add the grated tomato and stir well. Cook over low heat until the mixture has thickened. Process the contents of the saucepan in a food processor or blender; push the mixture through a fine sieve into a clean saucepan. Cook this purée until it has reduced to 200 ml (scant 1 cup). Set aside.

To make the paella rice, preheat the oven to 150°C/300°F/Gas Mark 2. Heat the Langoustine Oil in the paella pan over low heat, add the squid, sprinkle with salt and sauté for a few minutes until lightly brown and any liquid has evaporated. Add the rice and cook over low heat for a few minutes, stirring, until thoroughly coated and translucent; do not allow it to burn. Add 200 ml (scant 1 cup) sofrito and stir well. Add the paprika, stir through and cook over moderate heat for a few seconds, taking care that it does not burn. Pour in the fumet.

Bring to a boil over medium heat, add the saffron, morels and lime zest and cook for 5 minutes, until the rice rises to the surface of the liquid. Taste and season with salt if necessary, bearing in mind that the flavours will become more pronounced as the liquid evaporates.

Put the paella in the preheated oven for 9 minutes. Remove it from the oven and arrange the langoustines over the rice. Put the paella back in the oven for 3 minutes. Remove the paella from the oven once again, allow it to rest for 3 minutes, then serve.

PAELLA RICE WITH PRAWNS (SHRIMP), RED MULLET AND WHITE TRUFFLE

Serves 2
Preparation: 40 minutes
(excluding fumet and stock) +
2 hours for draining
Cooking: 17 minutes

1 large aubergine (eggplant)

3 tablespoons coarse sea salt

600 ml (2½ cups) red mullet fumet (see Rock Fish Fumet, page 49; make it with the heads, bones and trimmings of the red mullets used in this recipe)

500 ml (2¼ cups) Garlic Oil (page 60) or ordinary olive oil

150 g (5 oz) small raw prawns (shrimp), shelled and heads removed

200 g (3½ cups) spring onions (scallions), finely diced

100 g (¾ cup) courgette (zucchini), finely diced

1 clove garlic, finely chopped

200 g (1 cup) bomba or other short-grain rice

2 red mullets or other mullet or firm white fish, filleted, reserving the livers and trimmings (including the heads and bones)

200 ml (scant 1 cup) Prawn (Shrimp) and Red Mullet Stock (page 44)

½ teaspoon Spanish sweet smoked paprika

¼ teaspoon saffron threads, toasted and pounded

white truffle

salt and pepper

Fresh white truffles, like black truffles, will keep for several days in the refrigerator in an airtight container. The truffle needs to come into direct contact with the rice so that the rice can absorb its flavour.

For an extra-fine texture, use a 41-cm (16-inch) paella pan suitable for use on the stove and in the oven.

Hold the aubergine (eggplant) with a fork over the flame of the stovetop, or under a very hot grill (broiler), until the skin is completely black. Wrap it in aluminium foil, prick a few holes into it and set aside to drain in a strainer set over a bowl to catch any liquid. After 2 hours, remove the foil and scrape the flesh away from the skin with a spoon, and reserve it.

Heat the fumet but do not allow it to boil. Preheat the oven to 150°C/300°F/Gas Mark 2.

Heat the Garlic Oil in the paella pan over low heat, add the prawns (shrimp) and sauté briefly without cooking them through. Set the prawns aside on a plate, covered with aluminium foil. Add the spring onions, courgettes (zucchini) and aubergine to the paella pan and sauté for a few minutes until lightly browned and softened, then add the chopped garlic and sauté briefly.

Add the rice and cook over low heat for a few minutes, stirring with a wooden spatula, until thoroughly coated and translucent; do not allow the rice to burn. Add the red mullet livers, followed by the Prawn (Shrimp) and Red Mullet Stock, stirring and deglazing the pan by scraping up any bits from the bottom of the pan with a wooden spatula.

Add the smoked paprika, stir through and cook over moderate heat for a few seconds, taking care it does not burn. Pour in the hot red mullet stock, stir and bring to a boil. Add the saffron. If you have a timer, set it to 17 minutes. Cook over high heat for 5 minutes, until the rice rises to the surface of the liquid. Taste, adding salt, if necessary, bearing in mind that the flavours will become more pronounced as the liquid evaporates. Put the paella in the preheated oven for 8 minutes.

Remove the paella from the oven and allow it to rest for 3 minutes. Using a mandolin or a truffle grater, slice the truffle into wafer thin slices and sprinkle these shavings over the top of the rice.

PAELLA RICE WITH SALT COD, GARLIC, APPLE AND CAULIFLOWER

Serves 2
Preparation time: 20 minutes
(excluding stock) + 24 hours
for soaking
Cooking time: 17 minutes

400 ml (1¾ cups) Salt Cod Stock
(page 39)

100 ml (scant ½ cup) Garlic Oil (see
page 60) or ordinary olive oil

300 g (11 oz) salt cod (or frozen de-
salted cod, thawed)

1 bunch garlic shoots

150 g (5 oz) cauliflower, broken up
into florets and cut into 2-cm (¾-inch)
lengths

200 g (1 cup) bomba or other short-
grain rice

150 g (⅔ cup) Tomato Sofrito no. 2
(page 54) or passata (puréed
canned tomatoes)

½ teaspoon Spanish sweet
smoked paprika

¼ teaspoon saffron threads, toasted
and pounded

30 g (1¼ oz) Fogón-style Olives
(page 57)

1 Reinette, Cox's Orange Pippin or Cox
apple, peeled, cored and cut into thin
slices

30 g (½ cup) spring onion (scallion),
green part only, finely chopped

salt

Salt cod has to be soaked for 24 hours to get rid of the salt, but you can also buy it frozen and ready to use (de-salted).

For an extra-fine texture, use a 41-cm (16-inch) paella pan suitable for use on the stove and in the oven.

The day before, soak the salt cod in cold water; change the water several times over the next 24 hours.

Heat the Salt Cod Stock but do not allow it to boil. Preheat the oven to 150°C/300°F/Gas Mark 2.

Heat the Garlic Oil in the paella pan over low heat, add the salt cod and sauté lightly, skin side down, for a few minutes. When it has lightly browned, add the garlic shoots and cauliflower and sauté for several minutes. Take the cod out of the pan and put it into a dish, covered with aluminium foil.

Continue to heat the liquid released by the fish for several minutes until it has evaporated. Add the rice and cook over low heat for a few minutes, stirring with a wooden spatula, until thoroughly coated and translucent; do not allow the rice to burn. Add the Tomato Sofrito no. 2 and stir well, deglazing the pan by scraping up any bits on the bottom of the pan with a wooden spatula.

Add the paprika, stir through and cook over moderate heat for a few seconds, taking care that it does not burn. Pour in the hot Salt Cod Stock and bring to a boil over moderate heat. If you have a timer, set it to 17 minutes. Add the saffron and olives and cook for 5 minutes until the rice rises to the surface of the liquid. Taste and season with salt, if necessary, bearing in mind that the flavours will become more pronounced as the liquid evaporates. Arrange the salt cod and the apple slices attractively on top of the rice. Put the paella in the preheated oven for 12 minutes.

Remove the paella from the oven and allow it to rest for 3 minutes. Sprinkle the chopped spring onion all over the top and serve.

PAELLA RICE WITH BABY SQUID AND SAFFRON MILK-CAP MUSHROOMS

Serves 2
Preparation time: 20 minutes
(excluding fumet)
Cooking time: 17 minutes

500 ml (2¼ cups) Fish Fumet (page 48)

100 ml (scant ½ cup) Garlic Oil
(page 60) or ordinary olive oil

400 g (14 oz) baby squid, cleaned

300 g (11 oz) saffron milk-cap
(*Lactarius sanguifluus*) mushrooms,
cleaned and rinsed

200 g (1 cup) bomba or other short-
grain rice

100 ml (scant ½ cup) Cuttlefish Stock
(page 41)

½ teaspoon Spanish sweet
smoked paprika

¼ teaspoon saffron threads, toasted
and pounded

50 g (1 cup) spring onions (scallions),
green part only, finely chopped

salt

Use a 41-cm (16-inch) paella pan suitable for use on the stove and in the oven.

Heat the Fish Fumet but do not allow it to boil. Preheat the oven to 150°C/300°F/Gas Mark 2.

Heat the Garlic Oil in the paella pan over moderate heat, add the squid and sauté for a few minutes until golden brown and their juices evaporate. Add the mushrooms and sauté for several minutes until the mushrooms are browned.

Add the rice and cook over low heat for a few minutes, stirring with a wooden spatula, until thoroughly coated and translucent; do not allow the rice to burn. Add the Cuttlefish Stock and stir well, deglazing the pan by scraping up any bits on the bottom of the pan with a wooden spatula.

Add the paprika, stir through and cook over moderate heat for a few seconds, taking care that it does not burn. Pour in the hot fumet and stir in the saffron. Spread the rice and mushrooms out evenly in the paella pan and bring to a boil. If you have a timer, set it to 17 minutes. Taste and season with salt, if necessary, bearing in mind that the flavours will become more pronounced as the liquid evaporates. Cook for 5 minutes until the rice rises to the surface of the liquid. Make sure the ingredients are distributed evenly in the paella pan. Put the paella in the preheated oven for 12 minutes.

Remove the paella from the oven and allow it to rest for 3 minutes. Sprinkle the chopped spring onions (scallions) over the paella and serve.

HITE PAELLA RICE WITH SALT COD

ves 2
paration time: 25 minutes
cluding stock) + 24 hours soaking
king time: 17 minutes

ml (2 cups) Salt Cod Stock
ge 39)

ml (1¼ cups) rapeseed (canola)
grapeseed oil

unch fresh sage leaves

ml (¼ cup) olive oil

g (2 oz) salt cod skin, de-salted,
led and rinsed

g (5 oz) salt cod tripe (such as liver
swim bladder)

g (1¾ oz) spring onions (scallions),
into thin strips

g (11 oz) morel mushrooms,
aned carefully and dried

g (1 cup) bomba or other short-
in rice

ml (¼ cup) rice vinegar

easpoon Spanish sweet
oked paprika

To prepare the salt cod skin, soak a piece of salt cod for 24 hours in cold water, changing the water a couple of times. Remove and scrape the skin to remove the scales, then lift off the skin, and rinse and drain it. Use the salt cod flesh for another recipe.

For a moist texture, use a 34-cm (13½-inch) paella pan suitable for use on the stove and in the oven.

Heat the Salt Cod Stock but do not allow it to boil. Preheat the oven to 150°C/300°F/Gas Mark 2. Heat the rapeseed (canola) oil in a large pan and fry the fresh sage leaves for a few minutes, until crispy. Remove and drain on paper towels.

Heat the olive oil in the paella pan over low heat, add the salt cod skin and tripe and sauté for a few minutes until lightly browned. Remove them and allow any liquid to evaporate. Add the spring onions (scallions) and morel mushrooms and brown them for a few minutes over high heat.

Add the rice and cook over low heat for a few minutes, stirring with a wooden spatula, until thoroughly coated and translucent; do not allow the rice to burn. Add the rice vinegar and deglaze by stirring with a wooden spatula to dislodge any bits stuck to the bottom of the pan. Add the paprika, stir through and cook for a few seconds, taking care that it does not burn. Pour in the hot Salt Cod Stock and return the cod tripe to the pan. Bring to a boil. If you have a timer, set it to 17 minutes. Cook over moderate heat.

After 5 minutes the rice should rise to the surface of the liquid. Taste and season with a little salt, if necessary, bearing in mind that the ingredients are already somewhat salty and the flavours will become more pronounced as the liquid evaporates. Put the paella in the preheated oven for 12 minutes.

Remove the paella from the oven and allow it to rest for 3 minutes. Sprinkle the surface with the fried sage leaves and serve.

ARROZ EN PAELLA DE LANGOSTA « ALLER-RETOUR » A COLOMBO
'RETURN TO COLOMBO' PAELLA RICE WITH LOBSTER

Serves 2
Preparation time: 30 minutes
Cooking time: 17 minutes

1 live lobster, about 800 g (1¾ lb)

100 ml (scant ½ cup) Garlic Oil
(page 60) or ordinary olive oil

2 fresh chilli peppers

1 onion, finely chopped

½ green plantain (a type of savoury
banana), peeled and finely diced

4 spring onions (scallions),
finely chopped

200 g (7 oz) chayotes (chokos), peeled
and finely diced

½ green bell pepper, seeded, peeled
and finely diced

1 young turnip, finely diced

200 g (1 cup) bomba or other short-
grain rice

100 ml (scant ½ cup) dark Navy rum

½ teaspoon poudre de Colombo
(Caribbean curry powder)

1 lime

¼ teaspoon saffron threads, toasted
and pounded

salt

For a moist texture, use a 34-cm (13½-inch) paella pan suitable for use on the stove and in the oven.

Preheat the oven to 150°C/300°F/Gas Mark 2. Hold the lobster firmly, legs downwards, on the work surface; using a heavy, very sharp kitchen knife, insert the tip into its head, midway between the eyes and cut the head lengthwise in half, bringing the knife firmly but gently down along the middle of the shell, and cutting the whole lobster into two equal halves. Remove the leathery, gritty stomach sac from the head and the black intestinal tract from the centre of the body and discard them. Retrieve all the liquid released by the lobster and set aside; crush the claws and legs but leave these attached to the two halves of the lobster. Set aside. Heat 500 ml (2¼ cups) water.

Heat the Garlic Oil and the chilli peppers in the paella pan over low heat. Add the lobster halves, placing them flesh side downwards. Sprinkle with a little salt and sauté for a few minutes until lighted brown and the lobster has changed colour. Turn the two halves over and set aside in a deep dish; cover with aluminium foil.

Add the onion, plantain, spring onions, chayotes, green bell pepper and turnip to the ingredients left behind in the paella pan and sauté for several minutes until lightly browned and softened.

Add the rice and cook over low heat for a few minutes, stirring with a wooden spatula, until thoroughly coated and translucent; do not allow the rice to burn. Pour in the rum and deglaze the bottom of the pan by scraping up any bits on the bottom of the pan with a wooden spatula. Add the Caribbean curry powder, stir through and cook over moderate heat for a few seconds, making sure that it does not catch and burn. Remove the chilli peppers at this stage if you do not like very spicy flavours.

Pour in the hot water and finely grate the lime zest directly over the surface of the liquid. Bring to a boil. If you have a timer, set it to 17 minutes. Add the saffron and cook over very high heat for 5 minutes, until the rice rises to the surface of the liquid. Taste and add any salt if necessary, bearing in mind that the flavours will become more pronounced as the liquid evaporates. Place the two halves of the lobster on the surface of the paella, flesh side downwards. Put the paella in the preheated oven for 12 minutes.

Remove the paella from the oven and allow it to rest for 3 minutes before serving.

PAELLA RICE WITH LANGOUSTINES AND CEP (PORCINI) MUSHROOMS

Serves 2
Preparation time: 20 minutes
(excluding fumet)
Cooking time: 17 minutes

600 ml (2½ cups) Langoustine and Mushroom Fumet (page 46; use the trimmings from this recipe's mushrooms and langoustines for this)

4 langoustine tails, about 100 g (3½ oz) each

50 ml (¼ cup) Mushroom Oil (page 61) or ordinary olive oil

200 g (7 oz) baby cuttlefish, weighing 20 g (¾ oz) each, cleaned

200 g (7 oz) fresh cep (porcini) mushrooms, washed, dried and chopped

2 spring onions (scallions), finely chopped

200 g (1 cup) bomba or other short-grain rice

200 g (⅔ cup) Tomato Sofrito (page 54) or passata (puréed canned tomatoes)

½ teaspoon Spanish sweet smoked paprika

¼ teaspoon saffron threads, toasted and pounded

1 lime

salt and pepper

I suggest you serve a salad of small, raw cep (porcini) mushroom, dressed in a lemon vinaigrette with this paella. Wash the mushrooms thoroughly, dry them and slice them very thinly. Put them in a salad bowl. Just before sitting down to eat, sprinkle them with a little salt and dress them with the vinaigrette, made with Citrus-flavoured Oil (see page 60). Sprinkle with plenty of pepper and serve with the paella.

For a moist texture, use a 34-cm (13½-inch) paella pan suitable for use on the stove and in the oven.

Heat the Langoustine and Mushroom Fumet but do not allow it to boil. Preheat the oven to 150°C/300°F/Gas Mark 2.

Slit the bodies of the langoustines, starting at the tail end and stopping short of their heads. Remove the black intestinal tract. Set them aside.

Heat the Mushroom Oil in the paella pan over moderate heat, add the baby cuttlefish and sauté for a few minutes until lightly browned all over and the liquid they release evaporates. Add the mushrooms and spring onions and sauté for several minutes until lightly browned, and all the liquid has evaporated.

Add the rice and cook over low heat for a few minutes, stirring with a wooden spatula, until thoroughly coated and translucent; do not allow the rice to burn. Add the Tomato Sofrito and stir well, deglazing the pan by scraping up any bits on the bottom of the pan with a wooden spatula.

Add the paprika, stir through and cook over moderate heat for a few seconds, taking care that it does not burn. Pour in the hot fumet, stir and bring to a boil. Add the saffron, and finely grate half the lime zest, allowing it to fall directly into the pan. If you have a timer, set it to 17 minutes. Allow to cook over very high heat for 5 minutes until the rice rises to the surface of the liquid. Taste and season with salt, if necessary, bearing in mind that the flavours will become more pronounced as the liquid evaporates. Put the paella in the preheated oven for 9 minutes.

Remove it from the oven, arrange the langoustines attractively on top of it and return the paella to the oven for a further 3 minutes. Remove it from the oven again and allow the paella to rest for 3 minutes before serving.

ALICANTE–MARSEILLE RETURN' PAELLA RICE

Serves 2
Preparation time: 40 minutes
(excluding stock)
Cooking time: 17 minutes

300 g (11 oz) rock fish (such as mullet, gurnard or scorpion fish), filleted

600 ml (2½ cups) Bouillabaisse Stock (page 39)

1 potato

500 ml (2¼ cups) extra-virgin olive oil

1 dried ñora pepper, stalk and seeds removed, coarsely crumbled

1 clove garlic

100 g (3½ oz) cuttlefish, white part (mantle) only

100 g (3½ oz) fennel bulb, cut into very thin slices

200 g (1 cup) bomba or other short-grain rice

400 ml (1¾ cups) pastis

100 g (⅓ cup) Tomato Sofrito (page 54) or passata (canned puréed tomatoes)

½ teaspoon Spanish sweet smoked paprika

½ teaspoon saffron threads, toasted and pounded

salt

I created this recipe for a culinary event. Pastis played a leading role, not only as an ingredient in the paella but also as an aperitif while it was cooking. The Piquillo Pepper Rouille (page 37) was specially created for this paella: make sure you serve it as an accompaniment.

For an extra-fine texture, use a 41-cm (16-inch) paella pan suitable for use on the stove and in the oven.

Poach your chosen rock fish very gently in the Bouillabaisse Stock. You can serve these separately while your guests are waiting for the paella to finish cooking, or keep them hot, covered with aluminium foil, ready to serve with the paella. Steam the potato for 20 minutes over the pan of Bouillabaisse Stock. Strain the stock and keep it hot. Add enough hot water to the stock so you still have 600 ml (2½ cups). Preheat the oven to 150°C/300°F/Gas Mark 2.

Heat the oil in the paella pan over low heat, add the ñora pepper and garlic and gently sauté for a few minutes until lightly browned; do not allow them to burn. Remove them from the pan, put into a mortar and pound to a paste with a pestle. Set aside.

Add the cuttlefish flesh and fennel to the paella pan and sauté for a few minutes, turning them all the time, until they are lightly browned and the juices they release have evaporated.

Add the rice and cook over low heat for a few minutes, stirring with a wooden spatula, until thoroughly coated and translucent; do not allow the rice to burn. Pour in the pastis and deglaze the pan, scraping up any bits on the bottom of the pan with a wooden spatula. Add the ñora pepper and garlic paste, followed by the Tomato Sofrito, and stir to combine.

Add the paprika, stir through and cook over moderate heat for a few seconds, taking care that it does not burn. Pour in the hot stock, add the saffron and spread the rice out evenly in the pan. Bring to a boil. If you have a timer, set it to 17 minutes. Cook over very high heat for 5 minutes until the rice rises to the surface of the liquid. Taste and season with salt, if necessary, bearing in mind that the flavours will become more pronounced as the liquid evaporates.

Place the potato in the centre of the paella pan. Put the paella in the preheated oven for 12 minutes. Remove the paella from the oven and allow it to rest for 3 minutes before serving, preferably accompanied by a Piquillo Pepper Rouille.

PAELLA RICE WITH RED MULLET AND ROASTED PUMPKIN

Serves 2
Preparation time: 45 minutes
(excluding fumet) + 1 hour drying time
Cooking time: 17 minutes

400 g (14 oz) pumpkin or Hokkaido squash, cut into 3-cm (1¼-inch) cubes

500 ml (2¼ cups) Rock Fish Fumet (page 49, using mullet trimmings only)

200 ml (scant 1 cup) grapeseed or sunflower oil

3 sprigs rosemary

2 tablespoons pumpkin seed oil

1 clove garlic, finely chopped

200 g (7 oz) tomato, halved, seeded and grated, skin discarded

200 g (7 oz) pumpkin, cut into 5-mm (¼-inch) dice

150 ml (⅓ cup) dry sherry

50 ml (¼ cup) Garlic Oil (page 60) or ordinary olive oil

200 g (7 oz) spring onions (scallions), finely chopped

200 g (1 cup) bomba or other short-grain rice

8 small red mullets (or striped mullets), cleaned and scaled, with their livers

½ teaspoon Spanish sweet smoked paprika

¼ teaspoon saffron threads, toasted and pounded

50 g (2 cups) spinach leaves, washed, stalks removed and squeezed dry

salt

For an extra-fine texture, use a 41-cm (16-inch) paella pan suitable for use on the stove and in the oven.

Preheat the oven to 100°C/210°F/Gas Mark ¼. Boil the cubed pumpkin for 4–5 minutes in a pan of boiling salted water. Drain while it is still half-cooked and dry in the oven for 1 hour. Take the pumpkin out of the oven and allow to cool. Increase the oven temperature to 150°C/300°F/Gas Mark 2. Heat the Rock Fish Fumet without allowing it to boil.

Heat the grapeseed oil in a pan over low heat, add the sprigs of rosemary and sauté for a few minutes until they are crunchy. Take them out of the pan and set aside to drain on paper towels. One of these sprigs will be added to the sauce; the two others will decorate the paella when it is served.

To make the pumpkin sauce, heat the pumpkin seed oil over low heat, add the chopped garlic and gently sauté for a few minutes until it starts to colour. Add the grated tomato and the diced pumpkin. Scatter the leaves from one of the fried sprigs of rosemary into the pan and allow the contents of the pan to simmer over low heat for several minutes until it has reduced a little, and the pumpkin is tender. Pour in the sherry and deglaze the pan by scraping up any bits on the bottom of the pan with a wooden spatula. Push the contents of the pan through a fine-mesh sieve (strainer) and set aside.

Heat the Garlic Oil in the paella pan over moderate heat, add the spring onions (scallions) and sauté for a few minutes until lightly browned. Add the rice and cook over low heat for a few minutes, stirring with a wooden spatula, until thoroughly coated and translucent; do not allow the rice to burn. Add the red mullet livers, followed by the pumpkin sauce and stir with a spatula. Allow to cook for several minutes.

Add the paprika, stir through and cook over moderate heat for a few seconds, taking care it doesn't burn. Pour in the hot Rock Fish Fumet, stir and bring to a boil. Add the dried cubed pumpkin and the saffron. Bring to a boil. If you have a timer, set it to 17 minutes. Cook over moderate heat for 5 minutes until the rice rises to the surface of the liquid. Taste and season with salt, if necessary, bearing in mind that the flavours will become more pronounced as the liquid evaporates.

Add the spinach leaves, then put the paella in the oven for 8 minutes. Remove the paella from the oven, arrange the red mullet on top of the rice and return the paella to the oven for a further 4 minutes. Remove the paella from the oven again and allow it to rest for 3 minutes. Garnish with the two remaining fried rosemary sprigs and serve.

ARROZ EN PAELLA ARGENTANESE
ARGENTAN-STYLE PAELLA RICE

Serves 2
Preparation time: 25 minutes
(excluding stock)
Cooking time: 17 minutes

600 ml (2½ cups) Chicken or Rabbit Stock (page 51)

50 ml (¼ cup) Garlic Oil (page 60) or ordinary olive oil

120 g (4 oz) boneless free-range chicken, cut into 30-g (1-oz) pieces

80 g (1⅓ cups) spring onions (scallions), cut into thin strips

80 g (⅔ cup) turnips, diced

½ green bell pepper, seeded, peeled and cut into thin strips

2 tablespoons shredded white cabbage

200 g (1 cup) bomba or other short-grain rice

Reinette, Cox's Orange Pippin or Fox apple, peeled and cut into 2-cm (¾-inch) dice

100 ml (scant ½ cup) Normandy dry (hard) cider

100 g (⅔ cup) Tomato Sofrito (page 54) or passata (puréed canned tomatoes)

½ teaspoon Spanish sweet smoked paprika

120 g (4 oz) confit beef tripe, cut into 30-g (1-oz) pieces

1 teaspoon saffron threads, toasted and pounded

Salt

This paella takes its name from Argentan, a town in Normandy, northern France. I created it in February 2009 with local ingredients for a cookery demonstration held during a Spanish Day organized by the Université Populaire du Goût.

For a moist texture, use a 34-cm (13½-inch) paella pan suitable for use on the stove and in the oven.

Heat the Chicken or Rabbit Stock but do not allow it to boil. Preheat the oven to 150°C/300°F/Gas Mark 2.

Heat the Garlic Oil in the paella pan over low heat. Keeping the heat low, add the chicken pieces to the pan and sauté for several minutes until browned all over. Add the vegetables and sauté for several minutes until the vegetables are softened.

Add the rice and cook over low heat for a few minutes, stirring with a wooden spatula, until thoroughly coated and translucent; do not allow the rice to burn. Add the diced apple. Pour in the cider and deglaze the pan by scraping up any bits on the bottom of the pan with a wooden spatula. Add the Tomato Sofrito, stir well and continue to cook until the mixture has reduced and thickened.

Add the paprika, stir through and cook over moderate heat for a few seconds, taking care that it does not burn. Pour in the hot Chicken or Rabbit Stock and bring to a boil. Add the tripe pieces. If you have a timer, set it to 17 minutes. Add the saffron. Cook over very high heat for 5 minutes until the rice rises to the surface of the liquid. Taste and season with salt, if necessary, bearing in mind that the flavours will become more pronounced as the liquid evaporates.

Distribute the pieces of tripe evenly on top of the rice. Put the paella in the preheated oven for 12 minutes. Remove the paella from the oven, allow it to rest for 3 minutes, then serve.

ARROZ EN PAELLA DE JAMÓN IBÉRICO, VERDURAS Y FOIE GRAS
PAELLA RICE WITH IBÉRICO HAM, SPRING VEGETABLES AND FOIE GRAS

Serves 2
Preparation time: 25 minutes
(excluding stock and foie gras) +
24 hours for chilling
Cooking time: 17 minutes

For the salted foie gras

1 whole duck foie gras

2 kg (4½ lb) coarse sea salt

mixed ground spices: (white
pepper, ginger, white cardamom,
coriander seeds)

For the paella rice

600 ml (2½ cups) Ibérico Ham Stock
(page 50)

500 ml (2¼ cups) Ibérico Ham-
flavoured Oil (page 62) or ordinary
olive oil

2 small carrots

2 small turnips

200 g (7 oz) spring onions (scallions),
cut into fine strips

½ bunch green asparagus, woody
ends removed, stems peeled and tips
kept intact

50 g (⅓ cup) broad (fava) beans,
shelled, blanched and outer
skins removed

50 g (⅓ cup) fresh peas, shelled
and blanched

1 clove garlic, finely chopped

200 g (1 cup) bomba or other short-
grain rice

200 g (⅔ cup) Tomato Sofrito (page 54)
or passata (puréed canned tomatoes)

½ teaspoon Spanish sweet
smoked paprika

¼ teaspoon saffron threads, toasted
and pounded

150 g (5 oz) Ibérico ham, very
thinly sliced

salt

This paella goes wonderfully well with foie gras. Franck Cerruti, chef at the Louis XV restaurant in Monte Carlo (an Italian by birth) maintains that the practice of adding a little butter to a risotto when it is cooked originated with a Flemish tercio, a company of mercenaries fighting for the Spanish King, who are said to have introduced this finishing touch to Naples in the sixteenth or seventeenth century. My idea was to replace the butter with foie gras, salted in the same way as the ham that flavours this paella. However, this paella is also delicious without the foie gras.

For a moist texture, use a 34-cm (13½-inch) paella pan suitable for use on the stove and in the oven.

Prepare the foie gras the day before. Remove as many of the veins as possible from the liver without breaking it up too much. Press it back into shape and wrap securely in 6 layers of muslin (cheese-cloth). Bury the wrapped liver in a bowl of coarse salt and mixed ground spices, place it in the refrigerator and leave it for 24 hours. Remove the salt and the muslin. Wrap the liver in clingfilm (plastic wrap) and chill it in the refrigerator until it is to be served.

To make the paella, heat the Ibérico Ham Stock but do not allow it to boil. Preheat the oven to 150°C/300°F/Gas Mark 2.

Heat the Ibérico Ham-flavoured Oil in the paella pan over moderate heat, add all the vegetables and sauté for 2 minutes. Add the garlic to the centre of the pan and sauté briefly.

Add the rice and cook over low heat for a few minutes, stirring with a wooden spatula, until thoroughly coated and translucent; do not allow the rice to burn. Add the Tomato Sofrito and stir well, deglazing the pan by scraping up any bits on the bottom of the pan with a wooden spatula.

Add the paprika, stir through and cook over moderate heat for a few seconds, taking care that it does not burn. Pour in the hot Ibérico Ham Stock, stir and bring to a boil. If you have a timer, set it to 17 minutes. Add the saffron and cook over high heat for 5 minutes until the rice rises to the surface of the liquid. Taste and season with salt, if necessary, bearing in mind that the flavours will become more pronounced as the liquid evaporates.

Put the paella pan in the preheated oven for 12 minutes. Remove the paella from the oven, allow it to rest for 3 minutes, then arrange the slices of ham over the rice. As they become warm the slices will almost melt on to the surface. Moments before serving the paella, cut the foie gras into 1-cm (½-inch) dice and add about 40 g (1½ oz) per serving.

NEW YORK-STYLE PAELLA RICE WITH SAUSAGES FROM AROUND THE WORLD

Serves 4
Preparation time: 25 minutes
(excluding stock)
Cooking time: 17 minutes

900 ml (3¾ cups) Ibérico Ham Stock (page 50)

your choice of 7 different types of sausage (such as Merguez sausage, Mexican chorizo, smoked sausage, Kielbasa, Asturian smoked sausage, Italian sausage, Frankfurters or Montbéliard sausage), thickly sliced

100 ml (scant ½ cup) Garlic Oil (page 60) or ordinary olive oil

200 g (2 cups) green beans, washed, trimmed and cut into 3–4-cm (1¼–2 inch) lengths

200 g (1½ cups) turnips, diced

200 g (2 cups) Savoy cabbage, finely shredded

400 g (2 cups) bomba or other short-grain rice

400 g (1⅓ cups) Tomato Sofrito (page 54) or passata (puréed canned tomatoes)

1 teaspoon Spanish sweet smoked paprika

60 g (⅓ cup) cooked haricot (navy) beans

½ teaspoon nam prik pao sauce (Thai chilli paste)

½ teaspoon saffron threads, toasted and pounded

100 g (1 cup) fresh mangetouts (snow peas), finely chopped

salt

I created this paella with the New York chef Daniel Boulud in mind, as a tribute to his restaurant, DBGB Kitchen and Bar. It can be served with ketchup, mustard or gherkins (pickles), or with any popular accompaniment to sausages.

For an extra-fine texture, use a 51-cm (20-inch) paella pan suitable for use on the stove and in the oven.

Heat the Ibérico Ham Stock but do not allow it to boil. Preheat the oven to 150°C/300°F/Gas Mark 2.

Put the sausages into a large pan of very gently boiling water and poach for a few minutes, until they release some of their fat. Drain them and set aside.

Heat the Garlic Oil in the paella pan over low heat, add the green beans, turnips, cabbage and sausages and sauté for a few minutes until the vegetables are softened.

Add the rice and cook over low heat for a few minutes, stirring with a wooden spatula, until thoroughly coated and translucent; do not allow the rice to burn. Add the Tomato Sofrito and mix well, deglazing the pan by scraping up any bits on the bottom of the pan with a wooden spatula.

Add the paprika, stir through and cook over moderate heat for a few seconds, taking care that it does not burn. Pour in the hot Ibérico Ham Stock. Add the cooked haricot (navy) beans and the nam prik pao sauce stir and bring to a boil over high heat. If you have a timer, set it to 17 minutes. Arrange the sausages evenly on the paella, add the saffron and cook over moderate heat for 5 minutes until the rice rises to the surface of the liquid. Taste the stock and season with salt, if necessary, bearing in mind that the flavours will become more pronounced as the liquid evaporates.

Put the paella in the preheated oven and cook for 12 minutes. Remove the paella from the oven and allow it to rest for 3 minutes. Sprinkle the mangetouts (snow peas) over the surface of the paella and serve.

ARROZ EN PAELLA BLANCA DE BONITO CON JAMÓN IBÉRICO
WHITE PAELLA RICE WITH BONITO AND IBÉRICO HAM

Serves 2
Preparation time: 30 minutes
(excluding stock)
Cooking time: 17 minutes

1 tablespoon olive oil

1 clove garlic

1 dried ñora pepper, stalk and seeds
removed, coarsely crumbled

400 ml (1¾ cups) Bonito Stock
(page 40)

1 bonito or tuna fillet, 4 cm (1½ inches)
in diameter

150 g (5 oz) Ibérico ham, cut into long,
thin strips

oil for frying, such as grapeseed or
sunflower oil

1 whole bok choy, the leaves separated
from the stem, and leaves and stem cut
into thin strips

50 ml (¼ cup) sesame oil

100 g (3½ oz) spring onions (scallions),
white parts cut into thin strips,
and green parts sliced separated
for garnishing

½ green bell pepper, seeded, peeled
and thinly sliced

50 ml (¼ cup) rice wine vinegar

200 g (1 cup) bomba or other short-
grain rice

50 ml (¼ cup) hon tsuyu sauce

½ teaspoon Spanish sweet
smoked paprika

8 g (¼ oz) dashi powder

salt

*For an extra-fine texture, use a 41-cm (16-inch) paella pan suitable
for use on the stove and in the oven.*

Heat the olive in a pan over low heat, add the garlic and ñora
pepper and sauté for a few minutes until the garlic is pale golden
brown. Put the garlic and ñora pepper into a mortar and pound
to a paste using a pestle. Set aside.

Heat the Bonito Stock but do not allow it to boil. Preheat the oven
to 150°C/300°F/Gas Mark 2.

Wrap the strips of Ibérico ham tightly around the bonito fillet,
secure and set aside. Heat the oil for deep-frying to 180°C/350°F,
or until a cube of bread browns in 30 seconds. Add the strips
of bok choy leaves and deep-fry briefly until crisp. Take them out
of the oil and drain on paper towels.

Heat the sesame oil in the paella pan over low heat and sauté the
prepared bonito fillet for a few minutes until browned all over.
Take the bonito out of the pan and set aside on a plate, covered
with aluminium foil. Add the vegetables to the paella pan and
sauté over moderate heat for about 5 minutes until softened. Add
the garlic and ñora pepper paste, pour in the rice wine vinegar
and deglaze the bottom of the pan by scraping up any bits on the
bottom of the pan with a wooden spatula. Allow to cook for several
minutes until all the liquid has evaporated.

Add the rice and and cook over low heat for a few minutes, stirring
with a wooden spatula, until thoroughly coated and translucent; do
not allow the rice to burn. Add the hon tsuyu sauce mix well and
deglaze the bottom of the pan again, scraping up any bits on the
bottom of the pan with the wooden spatula.

Add the paprika, stir through and cook over moderate heat for
a few seconds, taking care that it does not burn. Pour in the hot
Bonito Stock, stir and bring to a boil. Add the dashi powder. If
you have a timer, set it to 17 minutes. Cook over moderate heat
for 5 minutes until the rice rises to the surface of the liquid. Taste
and season with salt, if necessary, bearing in mind that the flavours will become more pronounced as the liquid evaporates. Put
the paella in the preheated oven for 9 minutes. Remove the paella
from the oven and place the ham-wrapped bonito on the rice. Put
the paella back in the oven for a further 3 minutes.

Remove the paella from the oven again and allow it to rest for
3 minutes. Sprinkle the paella with the fried bok choy leaves and
green onion rings. Cut the bonito roll into slices about 7 mm
(¼ inch) thick. Place a few of these slices on each plate. Serve.

'RETURN TO INDIA' PAELLA RICE

Serves 2
Preparation time: 25 minutes
(excluding stock)
Cooking time: 17 minutes

400 ml (1¾ cups) Chicken or Rabbit Stock (page 51)

50 ml (¼ cup) oil frying (e.g. grapeseed or sunflower oil)

200 g (7 oz) boneless chicken, cut into 30-g (1-oz) pieces

1 clove garlic, finely chopped

1 green bell pepper, seeded, peeled and sliced into thin strips

100 g (2 cups) spring onions (scallions), sliced into thin strips

50 g (½ cup) Savoy cabbage, sliced into thin strips

50 g (½ cup) courgette (zucchini), sliced into thin strips

4 cashew nuts

200 g (1 cup) bomba or other short-grain rice

3 tablespoons tamarind paste

2 teaspoons korma masala powder

1 tablespoon sultanas (golden raisins)

1 tablespoon grated fresh ginger

1 teaspoon curry powder (use more if desired)

100 ml (scant ½ cup) coconut milk

¼ teaspoon saffron threads, toasted and pounded

salt

For a moist texture, use a 34-cm (13½-inch) paella pan suitable for use on the stove and in the oven.

Heat the Chicken or Rabbit Stock but do not allow it to boil. Preheat the oven to 150°C/300°F/Gas Mark 2.

Heat the oil in the paella pan over moderate heat, add the chicken pieces and sauté for several minutes until browned all over. Push the chicken pieces to the side of the pan and add the garlic to the centre of the pan. As soon as the garlic begins to colour, add the vegetables and cashew nuts and cook for a few minutes until the vegetables begin to soften.

Add the rice and cook over low heat for a few minutes, stirring with a wooden spatula, until thoroughly coated and translucent; do not allow the rice to burn. Add the tamarind paste and the korma masala, scraping any bits off the bottom of the pan with a wooden spatula. Add the sultanas (golden raisins), grated ginger and the curry powder.

Pour in the very hot stock and the coconut milk. Spread the ingredients out evenly in the pan. Add the saffron and bring to a boil. If you have a timer, set it to 17 minutes. Cook over moderate heat for 5 minutes until the rice rises to the surface of the liquid. Taste and season with salt, if necessary, bearing in mind that the flavours will become more pronounced as the liquid evaporates.

Put the paella in the preheated oven for 12 minutes. Remove it from the oven, allow it to rest for 3 minutes, then serve.

RETURN TO HAVANA' *MOROS Y CRISTIANOS* PAELLA RICE

Serves 2
Preparation time: 25 minutes
(excluding stock)
Cooking time: 17 minutes

50 ml (¼ cup) olive oil

1 dried ñora pepper, stalk and seeds removed, coarsely crumbled

1 clove garlic, finely chopped

500 ml (2½ cups) stock and gravy from a stew (left-overs)

50 ml (¼ cup) Garlic Oil (page 60) or ordinary olive oil

1 Toulouse sausage, cut into small pieces

1 black pudding (blood sausage), cut into small pieces

100 g (3½ oz) salted pork belly (side), diced

50 g (½ cup) leek, white part only, sliced into 2-cm (¾-inch) rounds

50 g (½ cup) carrot, sliced into 2-cm (¾-inch) rounds

50 g (⅓ cup) turnip, diced

150 g (¾ cup) bomba or other short-grain rice

100 g (⅔ cup) Tomato Sofrito (page 54) or passata (puréed canned tomatoes)

1 teaspoon Spanish sweet smoked paprika

80 g (2¾ oz) canned black beans

1 teaspoon saffron threads, toasted and pounded

Salt

The classic dish of rice and beans is a staple of Spanish cooking, and nowhere more so than in Cuba, where the dish made with rice and black beans is known as moros y cristianos. *This was the inspiration for my paella.*

For a moist texture, use a 34-cm (13½-inch) paella pan suitable for use on the stove and in the oven.

Heat the olive oil in a frying pan or skillet over low heat, add the ñora pepper and garlic and gently sauté for a few minutes until the garlic clove is lightly browned. Put the garlic and ñora pepper into a mortar and pound to a paste with a pestle. Set aside. Heat the stock but do not allow it to boil. Preheat the oven to 150°C/300°F/Gas Mark 2.

Heat the Garlic Oil in the paella pan over moderate heat, add the Toulouse sausage and black pudding pieces and sauté until brown all over. Transfer them to a plate and cover with aluminium foil.

Add the pork belly (side) and vegetables to the paella pan and cook over moderate heat for several minutes until the vegetables have softened. Stir in the garlic and ñora pepper paste.

Add the rice and cook over low heat for a few minutes, stirring with a wooden spatula, until thoroughly coated and translucent; do not allow the rice to burn. Add the Tomato Sofrito and stir well, deglazing the pan by scraping up any bits on the bottom of the pan with a wooden spatula.

Add the paprika, stir through and cook over moderate heat for a few seconds, taking care that it does not burn. Pour in the hot stock, add the black beans, stir and bring to a boil. If you have a timer, set it to 17 minutes. Add the saffron and cook over very high heat for 5 minutes, until the rice rises to the surface of the liquid. Taste and season with salt, if necessary, bearing in mind that the flavours will become more pronounced as the liquid evaporates.

Arrange the Toulouse sausage and black pudding on top of the rice. Put the paella in the preheated oven for 12 minutes. Remove it from the oven, allow it to rest for 3 minutes, then serve.

PAELLA RICE WITH RABBIT AND SHERRY VINEGAR

Serves 2
Preparation time: 25 minutes
(excluding stock)
Cooking time: 17 minutes

400 ml (1¾ cups) Chicken or Rabbit Stock (page 51)

50 ml (¼ cup) Garlic Oil (page 60) or ordinary olive oil

1 clove garlic, finely chopped

300 g (11 oz) boneless, uncooked rabbit, cut into 30-g (1-oz) pieces

100 g (3½ oz) spring onions (scallions), cut into fine strips

200 g (1 cup) bomba or other short-grain rice

50 ml (¼ cup) best-quality sherry vinegar

100 g (⅓ cup) Tomato Sofrito (page 54) or passata (puréed canned tomatoes)

200 g (7 oz) snails, prepared, cooked and removed from their shells

½ teaspoon Spanish sweet smoked paprika

1 sprig rosemary

¼ teaspoon saffron threads, toasted and pounded

salt

For an extra-fine texture, use a 41-cm (16-inch) diameter paella pan suitable for use on the stove and in the oven.

Heat the Chicken or Rabbit Stock but do not allow it to boil. Preheat the oven to 150°C/300°F/Gas Mark 2.

Heat the Garlic Oil in the paella pan over low heat, add the garlic and sauté for a few minutes until lightly browned. Add the rabbit pieces to the pan and sauté for several minutes until browned all over. Push the rabbit pieces to the sides of the pan, add the spring onion (scallions) to the centre and sauté for a few minutes.

Add the rice and cook over low heat for a few minutes, stirring with a wooden spatula, until thoroughly coated and translucent; do not allow the rice to burn. Pour in the vinegar and deglaze the pan by scraping up any bits on the bottom of the pan with a wooden spatula. Add the Tomato Sofrito and stir well. Add the rosemary.

Add the paprika, stir through and cook over moderate heat for a few seconds, taking care that it does not burn. Add the hot Chicken or Rabbit Stock and the rosemary. Add the snails and spread these and the rabbit pieces out evenly in the pan. Add the saffron and bring to a boil. If you have a timer, set it to 17 minutes. Cook over very high heat for 5 minutes until the rice rises to the surface of the liquid. Taste and season with salt, if necessary, bearing in mind that the flavours will become more pronounced as the liquid evaporates. Remove and discard the rosemary.

Put the paella in the preheated oven for 12 minutes. Remove the paella from the oven, allow it to rest for 3 minutes, then serve.

ARROZ EN PAELLA « PARIS-PARIS »
'RETURN TO PARIS' PAELLA RICE

Serves 2
Preparation time: 25 minutes
Cooking time: 17 minutes +
25 minutes for the veal

1 boned veal shank, cut in half, each half rolled and tied as if for roasting

75 g (5 tablespoons) butter

50 g (heaping ⅓ cup) plain (all-purpose) flour, sifted

70 g (2½ oz) turnip, cut into matchsticks

70 g (2½ oz) carrot, cut into matchsticks

100 g (3½ oz) button mushrooms

200 g (1 cup) bomba or other short-grain rice

1 tablespoon Dijon mustard

100 ml (scant ½ cup) crème fraîche

salt

Here is a recipe that may look as if it does not belong here because it contains butter and crème fraîche, which are unusual ingredients in Mediterranean cooking. But since this book is all about a special cooking technique, there is no reason not to adapt it to different culinary traditions. Blanquette de veau (veal casserole) is routinely served in Parisian bistros, accompanied by plain rice and mushrooms. In this recipe the rice has the same texture as paella rice, enhanced by the flavour of the veal, mushrooms and mustard.

For an extra-fine texture, use a 41-cm (16-inch) paella pan suitable for use on the stove and in the oven.

Bring plenty of water to a boil in a large saucepan. Lower the veal into it, and when it returns to a boil, allow it to boil for a few minutes, then remove and drain it. Empty the saucepan and fill it with 2 litres (8¾ cups) of fresh water. Bring this water to a boil, season with a little salt and simmer the veal in it gently over very low heat for 25 minutes. When it is almost cooked, remove the veal from the saucepan and set aside. Boil the cooking water until it has reduced to 1 litre (4¼ cups). Strain this liquid through a fine-mesh sieve and keep hot. Preheat the oven to 150°C/300°F/Gas Mark 2.

Melt 50 g (4 tablespoons) of the butter in a casserole dish over low heat. Add the veal and sauté for several minutes, turning several times, but do not allow it to brown. Sprinkle it with the flour, cook for a few more minutes and then add the hot cooking stock. Bring to a boil over high heat and reduce the liquid to 500 ml (2¼ cups). Remove the veal and set it aside. Keep the cooking stock hot.

Melt the remaining butter in the paella pan over low heat, add the turnip, carrot and mushrooms and sauté for a few minutes until the vegetables begin to soften. Add the rice and cook over low heat for a few minutes, stirring with a wooden spatula, until thoroughly coated and translucent; do not allow the rice to burn. Add the mustard and stir well, deglazing the pan by scraping up any bits on the bottom of the pan with a wooden spatula.

Pour in the very hot stock and bring to a boil. If you have a timer, set it to 17 minutes. Stir the contents of the pan and spread them out evenly in the paella pan. Cook for 5 minutes, until the rice rise to the surface of the liquid. Taste and season with salt, if necessary, bearing in mind that the flavours will become more pronounced as the liquid evaporates. Add the cream and mix very thoroughly with the stock.

Add the veal to the pan and put the paella in the preheated oven for 12 minutes. Remove it from the oven, allow it to rest for 3 minutes, then serve.

ARROZ EN PAELLA CON VINO Y CODORNIZ
PAELLA RICE WITH RED WINE AND QUAILS

Serves 2
Preparation time: 35 minutes
(excluding stock)
Cooking time: 17 minutes

500 ml (1¾ cups) Quail Stock (page 51)

50 ml (¼ cup) Garlic Oil (page 60) or ordinary olive oil

2 quail, boned, filleted and legs removed (ask your butcher to give you the bones so you can make the stock)

1 clove garlic, finely chopped

200 g (2¼ cups) red cabbage, thinly sliced

50 g (⅓ cup) turnip, diced

50 g (scant ½ cup) carrots, cut into 2-mm (¼-inch) thick rounds

100 g (scant 1 cup) red onions, thinly sliced

200 ml (scant 1 cup) red wine

100 ml (scant ½ cup) sherry vinegar

200 g (1 cup) bomba or other short-grain rice

6 peeled sweet chestnuts

salt

It is important to make this rice dish in a stainless steel paella pan so that the ingredients retain their attractive violet colour.

For an extra-fine texture, use a 41-cm (16-inch) stainless steel paella pan suitable for use on the stove and in the oven.

Heat the Quail Stock but do not allow it to boil. Preheat the oven to 150°C/300°F/Gas Mark 2.

Heat the Garlic Oil in the paella pan over moderate heat, add the quail meat (except the legs) and sauté for several minutes until browned all over. Take them out of the pan and set aside, covered with aluminium foil.

Add the garlic, quail legs, red cabbage, turnips, carrots and onions and sauté over moderate heat for several minutes until softened. Pour in the wine and the vinegar and allow to reduce until there is hardly any liquid left in the pan.

Add the rice and cook over low heat for a few minutes, stirring with a wooden spatula, until thoroughly coated and translucent; do not allow the rice to burn.

Add the chestnuts. Pour in the very hot Quail Stock, stir and bring to a boil. If you have a timer, set it to 17 minutes. Cook over very high heat for 5 minutes until the rice rises to the surface of the liquid. Taste and season with salt, if necessary, bearing in mind that the flavours will become more pronounced as the liquid evaporates. Put the paella in the preheated oven. After 9 minutes, arrange the quail meat over the top of the paella and return it to the oven.

After 3 minutes, remove the paella from the oven. Allow it to rest for 3 minutes, then serve.

PAELLAS ON THE BARBECUE

COOKING PAELLA OUTSIDE

The following recipes are for paellas that are cooked outdoors, over a wood-burning or charcoal barbecue or grill. The fumet or stock is made in the paella itself. The water, therefore, needs to be added in two stages: the first by pouring in enough water to cook the rice, marking the water level with a folded strip of aluminium foil. Then a second quantity of liquid is added, which forms the stock, and this is left to evaporate until it returns to the level marked by the foil.

In these recipes, quantities and cooking times are only a guide. They can vary according to the intensity of your heat source and the type of rice chosen. Make a note of what works best for you to remember it for another time.

When making a paella outdoors, the *sofrito* is made in the pan in which the rice is cooked. As a result, the paella has a stronger flavour than if it had been cooked with water alone.

All the dried spices are used whole (seeds, stalks, sticks) and toasted in advance in a dry frying pan or skillet with no added oil. They are then placed in a muslin (cheesecloth) bouquet garni bag, so that their flavour can infuse directly into the liquid and rice of the paella.

THE EIGHT STAGES OF COOKING PAELLA ON A BARBECUE

Make sure that the paella pan is completely level throughout the cooking process, so that the level of the cooking liquid is even and the paella cooks evenly. When the heat of the wood or charcoal is fairly high, place the pan on a trivet or grill rack (or nearest to the heat source if your barbecue or grill can be regulated), pour in the olive oil and sauté the ingredients.

Add the vegetables, which require less cooking time than the meats, fish or other seafood. Continue adding ingredients in the order of how long they will take to cook. Next, push all the ingredients to the edge of the pan and add the grated fresh tomato. The oil will pool in the centre of the pan, which is exactly where you should put the tomato.

When the tomato is well fried, add the paprika and cook for a few seconds, taking care that it does not burn. To help prevent this, add the first quantity of water (enough to cook the rice) without delay. Indicate the water level with a strip of aluminium foil folded over the edge of the paella pan to mark the point to which the water comes. This is important: the aluminium foil marker shows how much liquid will be needed to finish cooking the rice.

④

Add the second quantity of liquid and bring to a boil. If desired, you can add a stock (bouillon) cube at this point.

⑤

After it has reduced a little and reached the level indicated on the foil marker, sprinkle the rice all over the surface of liquid in the pan, add the saffron and stir well. From this point onwards, leave the contents of the pan undisturbed. The rice has now started to 'set' and should stay put as it cooks until it is ready to be served.

⑥

After 5 minutes, taste, season with salt if needed and gradually reduce the heat (but do not allow to go off the boil completely). If you are using a trivet or grill rack, remove some of the embers under the pan or adjust the trivet or rack upwards so that the pan is positioned further away from the heat source. If you are cooking on a large, substantial barbecue or grill, move the pan to one side, where the heat is less intense.

⑦

Once you can see that the rice has started to absorb the liquid, reduce the heat and leave the paella to cook at an even gentler simmer. To regulate the heat, remove some of the embers under the pan or adjust the trivet or grill rack upwards so that the pan is further away from the heat source, or simply move the pan further away from the most intense heat if using a large barbecue.

⑧

Finish cooking the rice, allowing all the liquid that remains in the pan to evaporate. Taste to check whether the rice is cooked. If it is still a little too firm to the bite, carefully cover the rice with a clean, damp dish towel for 2–3 minutes and finish cooking. If it is definitely too firm, sprinkle a few tablespoons of very hot water over the surface of the rice and continue cooking until the rice is tender. If you want to make a *socarret*, or crust on the bottom of the pan, remove the dish towel and place the pan directly on the embers or over the hottest part of the barbecue; the paella will release a cloud of white steam; leave the pan in place until you detect a slight smell of burning. Remove the pan from the heat immediately.

PAELLA VALENCIANA
VALENCIAN PAELLA

Serves 6
Preparation time: 50 minutes
Cooking time: 17 minutes

600 g (1¼ lb) free-range farm-reared rabbit, with bones, or 1 duck, skin removed but not boned, cut into 40-g (1½-oz) pieces

800 g (1¾ lb) free-range chicken, skin removed but not boned, cut into 40-g (1½-oz) pieces

200 ml (scant 1 cup) olive oil

6 cloves garlic, unpeeled

150 g (5 oz) flat beans, trimmed

150 g (5 oz) green beans, trimmed

150 g (1 cup) cooked large haricot (navy) or butter (lima) beans (preferably Soissons or garrafón beans)

6 tender young artichokes, trimmed, stalks peeled if tough and cut into quarters

300 g (11 oz) tomatoes, halved, seeded and grated, skin discarded

1 teaspoon Spanish sweet smoked paprika

1 chicken stock (bouillon) cube or scant 1 tablespoon powdered chicken stock (bouillon) (optional)

600 g (3 cups) bomba or other short-grain rice

1½ teaspoons saffron threads, toasted and pounded

salt and pepper

Spices and flavourings

4 black peppercorns

4 Sichuan peppercorns

2 sprigs of rosemary

2 sprigs of sage

The ingredients for this paella can be varied according to the seasons and availability. In Valencia a flavourless food colouring powder is often used in place of saffron, but I prefer the distinctive aroma, flavour and beautiful orange-gold colour of pure saffron. I do recommend using Soissons haricot (navy) beans. In Spain, cooks would use garrafón beans, which are large white, slightly flattened butter (lima) beans.

As explained in the introduction, the traditional paella pan is made of polished carbon steel. When some vegetables – such as artichokes – come into contact with this metal, the resulting oxidation gives the rice a violet-tinged colour and a slightly metallic taste, both of which are characteristic of this recipe. For a moist texture, use a 60-cm (24-inch) paella pan.

Before starting to cook, preheat the barbecue or grill. Prepare the spices and flavourings. Lightly toast the black and Sichuan peppercorns in a dry frying pan or skillet until fragrant. Put them into a muslin (cheesecloth) bouquet garni bag with the rosemary and sage, and secure tightly. Set aside.

Recipe continues over

PAELLA VALENCIANA
VALENCIAN PAELLA

1. First, make sure that the paella pan is completely level, so that the paella cooks evenly. Season the rabbit or duck and the chicken pieces with salt and pepper. Heat 2 litres (8½ cups) water. Heat the olive oil in the paella pan over very high heat and sauté the garlic cloves. When the garlic is half cooked, add the rabbit or duck and the chicken pieces, and sauté until half cooked. Remove and discard the garlic.

2. Add the flat, green and haricot (navy) beans and artichokes, and sauté for a few minutes until starting to brown. Push the contents of the pan to one side, and add the tomato to the centre. Cook, stirring, until well fried, but do not allow the tomato to burn. Stir it into the other ingredients.

3. Add the paprika and quickly stir through, taking care that it does not burn; to prevent this, pour in 1.5 litres (6½ cups) of the hot water immediately, and add the bouquet garni bag of spices and flavourings.

4. Mark the water level with a strip of aluminium foil, folded over the edge of the paella pan. Add a further 500 ml (2¼ cups) water and the chicken stock (bouillon) cube or powder, if using, and stir to make sure it dissolves completely.

5. When the water has evaporated to the level of the marker, carefully sprinkle the rice into the pan, distributing it evenly. Add the saffron. Taste and season with salt if needed. Position all the ingredients in the pan as you want them to appear when the paella is served. Do not stir the rice again. Bring to a boil.

6. After 5 minutes, taste once more and season with salt if needed. Reduce the heat by removing some of the embers beneath the paella or by adjusting the trivet or grill rack upwards (or by moving the pan so that it sits over a place on the barbecue or grill where the heat is less intense). Remove and discard the bag of spices and flavourings.

7. When the rice starts to rise to the surface of the liquid, reduce the heat considerably, keeping the liquid at a gentle simmer. Do this by removing some of the embers under the pan or by adjusting the trivet or grill rack so that the pan is further away from the heat source (or by moving the pan to a cooler part of the barbecue or grill, or simply turning down the gas burners).

8. Finish cooking the rice, allowing all the liquid remaining in the pan to evaporate. Taste to check whether the rice is cooked: it should be tender but still very slightly firm to the bite. If it is a little too firm, cover the paella with a clean, damp dish towel for 2–3 minutes to finish cooking. If it is much too firm, sprinkle a few tablespoons of hot water on top of the rice and continue cooking until the rice is tender.

SEAFOOD PAELLA RICE

Serves 6
Preparation time: 50 minutes
Cooking time: 17 minutes

6 large king prawns (jumbo shrimp)

6 langoustines, about 80 g (2¾ oz) each

300 g (11 oz) uncooked small prawns (shrimp), peeled

1 scorpion fish, cleaned and filleted (skin on and bones reserved), each cut into 3 pieces

3 red mullet (or striped mullet), about 150 g (5 oz) each, cleaned, scaled and filleted (bones reserved)

200 ml (scant 1 cup) olive oil

3 cloves garlic, unpeeled

1 bay leaf

½ onion, cut into thick rings

3 ripe tomatoes, skinned, seeded and grated

1 teaspoon Spanish sweet smoked paprika

600 g (3 cups) bomba or other short-grain rice

1½ teaspoons saffron threads, toasted and pounded

6 grouper steaks, about 100 g (3½ oz) each

3 monkfish fillets, about 200 g (7 oz) each, halved and rinsed

300 g (11 oz) large fresh mussels, well scrubbed and rinsed, with beards removed

300 g (11 oz) large fresh clams, purged of any grit, scrubbed and rinsed

200 g (7 oz) fresh cockles, purged of any grit, scrubbed and rinsed

salt and pepper

Spices and flavourings

1 star anise

1 teaspoon pink peppercorns

1 teaspoon freeze-dried green peppercorns

1 teaspoon fennel seeds

1 teaspoon green anise seeds

½ liquorice stalk

10 g (¼ oz) fresh ginger, peeled

For a moist texture, use a 60-cm (24-inch) paella pan.

Preheat the barbecue or grill. Prepare the spices and flavourings. Lightly toast the star anise, pink and green peppercorns, fennel seeds and anise seeds in a dry frying pan or skillet over medium-high heat until fragrant. Put them into a muslin (cheesecloth) bouquet garni bag together with the liquorice stalk and ginger, and secure tightly. Set aside. Remove the heads from the king prawns (jumbo shrimp) and langoustines, and set aside with the prawns (shrimp). Rinse all the fish bones thoroughly and pat dry with paper towels.

Next, make sure that the paella pan is completely level to ensure that the paella cooks evenly. Heat the olive oil in the pan over very high heat, positioning it as close as possible to the heat source. Sauté the garlic and bay leaf for a few seconds. Add the onion, fish bones and all the shellfish heads. Sauté until lightly browned.

Add the tomatoes and cook, stirring, until thickened and reduced. Mix well into the other ingredients. Add the paprika and cook briefly for a few seconds more; do not allow to burn. Pour in 1.2 litres (5 cups) water, and add the bouquet garni bag of spices and flavourings. Mark the level of the liquid at this point using a strip of aluminium foil folded over the edge of the pan. Add another 500 ml (2¼ cups) water and bring to a boil.

When the water has evaporated and fallen to the level of the foil marker, remove the onion, garlic, fish bones and shellfish heads used to make the fumet, leaving all the precious liquid behind in the pan. Sprinkle the rice over the surface of the liquid in the pan, add the saffron and stir well. From this point onwards, leave the rice to cook totally undisturbed. Bring to a boil.

After 5 minutes, taste and season with salt, if needed, bearing in mind that the flavour will become more pronounced as the liquid evaporates. Reduce the heat by removing some of the embers under the pan or adjusting the trivet or grill rack so that the pan is further away from the heat source. Remove and discard the bag of spices and flavourings. When the rice begins to rise to the surface, reduce the heat further so that it maintains a very gentle simmer. This is done by removing some of the embers under the pan or by raising the trivet or grill rack so that the pan is further away from the heat source. Arrange the fish and seafood on the rice.

Finish cooking the rice, allowing all the fumet left in the pan to evaporate. Taste to check whether the rice is cooked: it should be tender but still very slightly firm to the bite. If it is little too firm, cover the paella with a clean, damp dish towel for 2–3 minutes to finish cooking. If it is much too firm, sprinkle a few tablespoons of hot water on top of the rice and continue cooking until the rice is tender. Remove from the heat and serve immediately.

PAELLA RICE WITH SPRING VEGETABLES

Serves 6
Preparation time: 40 minutes
Cooking time: 17 minutes

100 g (scant 1 cup) shelled fresh broad (fava) beans

100 ml (scant ½ cup) olive oil

12 baby artichokes, trimmed and stalks peeled

200 g (7 oz) baby carrots, tops trimmed off

100 g (¾ cup) cauliflower, broken into florets

300 g (2¾ cups) courgettes (zucchini), cut into large matchsticks

200 g (7 oz) large spring onions (scallions) or very young, small mild onions, trimmed

100 g (7 oz) garlic shoots or ordinary spring onions (scallions), trimmed

1 long, tender-skinned green sweet pepper, seeded and cut into fine strips

100 g (⅔ cup) fresh shelled green peas

2 cloves garlic, finely chopped

600 g (1 lb 5 oz) spinach (stalks removed)

4 tomatoes, halved, seeded and grated, skin discarded

1 teaspoon Spanish sweet smoked paprika

1 bouquet garni with bay leaf, thyme, rosemary, garlic, oregano

1 vegetable stock (bouillon) cube

1½ teaspoons saffron threads, toasted and pounded

600 g (3 cups) bomba or other short-grain rice

salt and pepper

Spices and flavourings

3 green cardamom pods

1 teaspoon caraway seeds

1 teaspoon cumin seeds

1 teaspoon black peppercorns

1 stick liquorice root

scant 1 teaspoon green anise seeds

1 cinnamon stick

1 star anise

For a moist texture, use a 60-cm (24-inch) paella pan.

Preheat the barbecue or grill. Prepare the spices and flavourings: lightly toast the spices in a dry frying pan or skillet until fragrant. Put them into a muslin (cheesecloth) bouquet garni bag and secure tightly. Blanch the broad (fava) beans in boiling water for a few seconds, then refresh under running cold water and peel off their skins (they should slip off easily). Set aside.

Make sure that the paella pan is completely level to ensure that the paella cooks evenly. Heat the olive oil in the pan over high heat (or position the pan as close as possible to the heat source). Sauté all the vegetables, starting with those that require the most cooking time: artichokes, carrots, cauliflower, courgettes (zucchini), spring onions (scallions), garlic shoots, green pepper, peas, broad (fava) beans and spinach leaves.

Once all the vegetables have lightly browned, push them towards the edge of the pan, add the garlic to the centre and sauté until half-cooked. Next, add the grated tomato to the centre of the pan and cook, stirring, until thickened and reduced. Add the paprika, cook for a few seconds more and stir through all the ingredients until well mixed. Pour in 1.5 litres (6 ⅓ cups) water, bring to a boil and cook for 1 minute. Add the bouquet garni bag of spices and the bouquet garni of herbs. Dissolve the stock (bouillon) cube in the liquid, and add the saffron. Sprinkle the rice into the pan. Spread out all the ingredients evenly in the pan and cook over very high heat. Taste and season with salt, if needed.

After 5 minutes, taste once more and adjust the seasoning. Reduce the heat by removing some of the embers beneath the paella or by adjusting the trivet or grill rack upwards. Remove and discard the bags of spices and herbs. When the rice begins to rise to the surface of the liquid, reduce the heat under the pan to as low as possible, to maintain a gentle simmer.

Finish cooking the rice, allowing all the stock remaining in the pan to evaporate. Taste to check whether the rice is cooked: it should be tender, but still very slightly firm to the bite. If it is a little too firm, cover paella with a clean, damp dish towel for 2–3 minutes to finish cooking. If it is definitely not yet cooked through, sprinkle a few tablespoons of hot water over the rice and continue cooking until tender.

If you want to make a socarret, or crust on the bottom of the pan, place the pan directly on the embers or over the hottest part of the barbecue for 2 minutes. A fine layer of rice will stick to the bottom of the pan; this will have a crunchy texture, with no trace of bitterness. Remove the pan from the heat. Using a very sharp knife, very finely slice the reserved spinach stalks into 3-mm (¼-inch) rounds. Sprinkle all over the paella and serve immediately.

ARROZ EN PAELLA BLANCA DE SETAS DE OTOÑO
'WHITE' PAELLA RICE WITH AUTUMN (FALL) MUSHROOMS

Serves 6
Preparation: 40 minutes
Cooking: 17 minutes

2 kg (4½ lb) mixed mushrooms that require a long cooking time (such as ceps (porcini), chanterelles, shiitake or oyster mushrooms)

100 ml (scant ½ cup) olive oil

3 cloves garlic

2 sprigs of rosemary

pinch of Spanish sweet smoked paprika

600 g (3 cups) bomba or other short-grain rice

salt

Spices and flavourings

2 green cardamom pods

2 coriander seeds

2 sprigs of chervil

It is fun to gather wild mushrooms in the autumn (fall), filling your basket with lots of different fungi. Sometimes you find just a few specimens of many different species: this paella enables you to use up those that need prolonged cooking. All the flavours of the forest are found in this recipe, a delicious lunch dish to enjoy on your return from the fields. This recipe does not include the traditional sofrito, and so its stages of preparation differ from those found in other paellas.

For an extra-fine texture, use a 64-cm (25-inch) paella pan.

Preheat the barbecue or grill. Carefully wash the mushrooms under cold running water. Pat dry in a clean cloth or with paper towels. Check each mushroom to ensure that no traces of grit or impurities remain. Trim off the stalks from the cep (porcini) mushrooms if they are very long. Slice the mushrooms and set aside. Put the spices and the chervil into a muslin (cheesecloth) bouquet garni bag and secure tightly.

Make sure that the paella pan is completely level to ensure that the paella cooks evenly. Heat the olive oil in the paella pan over high heat, positioning it as close as possible to the heat source. Sauté the garlic cloves until lightly browned. Add the mushrooms and continue to sauté until half cooked. Push them towards the edge of the pan, and allow any liquid they have released to evaporate. Once only the oil remains, add the rosemary and sauté until crisp. Sprinkle the paprika over the mushrooms and sauté for a few seconds; do not allow it to burn.

Add the rice and sauté until translucent, stirring with a wooden spatula, without allowing it to burn. Mix together all the ingredients in the pan, then pour in 1.2 litres (5 cups) water. Bring to a boil over very high heat, positioning the pan as close as possible to the heat source. Add the bouquet garni bag.

After 5 minutes, taste and season with salt, bearing in mind that the flavours will become more pronounced as the liquid evaporates. Reduce the heat by removing some of the embers from beneath the pan or by adjusting the trivet or grill rack so that the pan is further away from the heat source (or by moving the pan to a cooler part of the barbecue or grill). Remove and discard the bag of spices.

Finish cooking the rice, allowing all the stock that is left in the pan to evaporate. Taste to check whether the rice is cooked: it should be tender but still a little firm to the bite. If it is little too firm, cover the paella with a clean, damp dish towel for 2–3 minutes to finish cooking. If it is much too firm, sprinkle a few tablespoons of hot water over the surface of the rice and continue cooking until the rice is tender. Serve immediately.

ARROZ EN PAELLA DE LANGOSTA
PAELLA RICE WITH LOBSTER

Serves 4
Preparation time: 30 minutes
Cooking time: 17 minutes

2 lobsters, about 500 g (1 lb 2 oz) each,
or 1 large lobster, about 1 kg (2¼ lb)

100 ml (scant ½ cup) olive oil

6 blanched almonds

2 cloves garlic

1 dried ñora pepper, stalk removed
and seeded

½ teaspoon saffron threads, toasted
and pounded

6 small sprigs of flat-leaf parsley

200 g (7 oz) squid, cleaned, prepared,
and cut into dice

3 tomatoes, halved, seeded and grated,
skin discarded

1 teaspoon Spanish sweet
smoked paprika

400 g (2 cups) bomba or other short-
grain rice

salt and pepper

Spices and flavourings

1 lemongrass stalk, tough outer layers
removed, cut into very thin rounds

2 scant tablespoons fennel seeds

5 coriander seeds

2 sprigs of lemon thyme

You can substitute spiny (rock) lobster or slipper lobster for ordinary lobster if desired.

For an extra-fine texture use a 51-cm (20-inch) paella pan.

Preheat the barbecue or grill. Lightly toast all the spices and flavourings in a dry frying pan or skillet over medium-high heat until fragrant. Put into a muslin (cheesecloth) bouquet garni bag and secure tightly. Cut the lobsters lengthwise into two equal halves. Remove the leathery, gritty stomach sac from their heads. If you are using only 1 lobster, separate the head from the tail. Cut the head in half lengthwise and slice the tail into large medallions. Retrieve all the liquid released from the lobster to use in the paella.

Make sure that the paella pan is completely level to ensure that the paella cooks evenly. Heat the olive oil in the paella pan over very high heat. Sauté the almonds, garlic cloves and ñora pepper until lightly browned. Remove with a slotted spoon, put into a mortar and pound with a pestle. Add the saffron and parsley, and pound with the pestle until you have a smooth paste. Set aside.

Season the lobsters with salt and place them in the pan, flesh side down. Sauté on both sides until half cooked. Remove from the pan and set aside. Next, gently sauté the squid briefly, then push it towards the edge of the pan. Add the grated tomato to the centre of the pan and cook, stirring, until thickened and reduced, making sure that it does not burn. Add the paprika and sauté for a few seconds more, taking care that it does not burn.

Add the reserved lobster liquid, 1 litre (4¼ cups) water and the muslin bag. Bring to a boil and sprinkle the rice as evenly as possible over the entire surface of the liquid. Let cook for 3 minutes, then place the lobsters on top of the rice, flesh side down. Cook over very high heat. Taste the fumet and season with salt, if necessary. Pour a little of the fumet into the mortar, and stir to thin the paste; pour this into the pan.

After 5 minutes, taste once more and adjust the amount of salt, if needed. Reduce the heat and remove and discard the bouquet garni bag. When the rice begins to rise to the surface, position the paella pan much further away from the heat source and continue cooking at a very gentle simmer.

Finish cooking the rice, allowing all the fumet that is left in the pan to evaporate. Taste to check whether the rice is cooked: it should be tender but still very slightly firm to the bite. If it is a little too firm, cover the paella with a clean, damp dish towel for 2–3 minutes to finish cooking. If it is much too firm, sprinkle a few tablespoons of hot water over the surface of the rice and continue cooking until the rice is tender.

PAELLA RICE WITH SPIDER CRAB AND PEAS

Serves 4
Preparation time: 40 minutes
Cooking time: 17 minutes

1 (or 2 small) spider crab, about
1.5 kg (3¼ lb)

100 g (3½) spring onions (scallions),
trimmed

100 ml (scant ½ cup) olive oil

2 cloves garlic

3 tomatoes, halved, seeded and grated,
skin discarded

1 teaspoon Spanish sweet
smoked paprika

5 basil leaves, enclosed in a muslin
(cheesecloth) bouquet garni bag

½ teaspoon saffron threads, toasted
and pounded

200 g (1½ cups) fresh shelled
green peas

400 g (2 cups) bomba or other short-
grain rice

salt

For a moist texture, use a 50-cm (20-inch) paella pan.

Preheat the barbecue or grill. First, clean the spider crab. Turn the crab on its back on a chopping board (cutting board) and plunge a sharp metal skewer or the tip of a very sharp knife through its head (just below its mouth parts) right through to the other side of the shell. Open the body and detach the legs (keeping them whole). Pick out all the meat from the shell and retrieve all the liquid within. Discard the tail and inedible parts (the feathery gills and the small, leathery stomach sac). Cut the central part of the body into two halves, and set all the edible parts of the crab aside. Cut the white part of the spring onions (scallions) into fine strips and set aside the green part.

Make sure that the paella pan is completely level to ensure that the paella cooks evenly. Heat the olive oil in the pan over very high heat. Sauté the garlic and chopped spring onions (scallions). Push to the edge of the pan and add the grated tomato. Reduce the heat by removing some of the embers under the pan or adjusting the trivet or grill rack so that the pan is further away from the heat source. Cook the tomato gently, stirring, until thickened and reduced.

Add the paprika, stir through and cook over low heat for 2 minutes. Pour in 1 litre (4¼ cups) water, bring to a boil and cook over very high heat for 1 minute. Add the bouquet garni bag containing the basil leaves. Next, add the reserved liquid from inside the crab and the meat from its body, then sprinkle in the saffron, bring to a boil and continue boiling for 4–5 minutes.

Add the peas, bring to a boil once more and sprinkle the rice as evenly as possible all over the liquid in the pan. Taste and season with salt, bearing in mind that the fumet should be a little bland at this stage because the crab will give it a far stronger flavour. Spread out all the ingredients, including the crab, evenly in the pan: the crab legs and shell should be in the centre, flesh side down. Remove and discard the bag of basil leaves. When the rice begins to rise to the surface, position the pan just far enough from the heat source to keep the contents at a very gentle simmer.

Finish cooking the rice, allowing all the fumet remaining in the pan to evaporate. Taste to check whether the rice is cooked: it should be tender but still very slightly firm to the bite. If it is a little too firm, cover the paella with a clean, damp dish towel for 2–3 minutes to finish cooking. If it is much too firm, sprinkle a few tablespoons of hot water over the surface of the rice and continue cooking until the rice is tender. Meanwhile, cut the green part of the spring onions into very fine rounds. Remove the pan from the heat, sprinkle over the spring onions and serve immediately.

PAELLA RICE WITH RABBIT AND SNAILS

Serves 4
Preparation time: 40 minutes
Cooking time: 17 minutes
(excluding stock)

100 ml (scant ½ cup) olive oil

1 oven-ready rabbit, boned and cut into 30-g (1-oz) pieces (reserve the bones)

3 sprigs of thyme

1 small sprig of rosemary, leaves picked

2 cloves garlic, finely chopped

1 dried ñora pepper, stalk and seeds removed, coarsely crumbled

1 tomato, halved, seeded and grated, skin discarded

1 kg (2¼ lb) snails, purged and cooked, shells discarded

100 ml (scant ¼ cup) good-quality sherry vinegar

1 teaspoon Spanish sweet smoked paprika

400 g (2 cups) bomba or other short-grain rice

1 litre (4¼ cups) Rabbit Stock (page 51)

½ teaspoon saffron threads, toasted and pounded

salt and pepper

For an extra-fine texture, use a 51-cm (20-inch) paella pan.

Preheat the barbecue or grill. Make sure that the paella pan is completely level to ensure that the paella cooks evenly. Heat the olive oil in the paella pan over medium-high heat or by positioning the pan close to the heat source. Sauté the rabbit with the thyme, rosemary, garlic and ñora pepper until the rabbit is browned all over, then take out the thyme, rosemary and garlic so that they do not burn. Push the meat towards the edge of the pan and add the grated tomato to the centre. Cook, stirring until starting to thicken and reduce, then add the snails and sherry vinegar. Finish reducing the tomato over low heat by removing some embers from underneath the pan or by positioning it far enough from the heat source for the contents to cook very gently. Add the paprika and cook for a few seconds more, stirring together all the ingredients thoroughly.

Add the rice and sauté for a few minutes, stirring with a wooden spatula, until thoroughly coated and translucent; do not allow to burn. Add the hot stock. Taste and season with salt. Arrange the rice and other ingredients attractively in the pan. They will stay where you put them until the paella is served – from now on, the rice should be left to cook undisturbed.

After 5 minutes, reduce the heat by removing some embers from under the pan or raising the trivet or grill rack so that the pan is further away from the heat source (or by moving the pan to a cooler part of the barbecue or grill). As soon as the rice rises to the surface, reduce the heat again so that the paella cooks very gently.

Finish cooking the rice, allowing all the remaining stock in the pan to evaporate. Taste to check whether the rice is cooked: it should be tender but still very slightly firm to the bite. If it is a little too firm, cover the paella with a clean, damp dish towel for 2–3 minutes to finish cooking. If it is much too firm, sprinkle a few tablespoons of hot water over the surface of the rice and continue cooking until the rice is tender. Allow to rest for 3 minutes before serving.

If you want to make a socarret, or crust on the bottom of the pan, remove the dish towel and place the pan directly on the embers or over the hottest part of the barbecue for 2 minutes. A thin layer of rice will stick to the bottom of the pan; the texture will be crunchy, with no trace of bitterness. Remove the pan from the heat and serve immediately.

ARROZ EN PAELLA DE CANGREJOS DE RÍO CON HIERBA LIMÓN
PAELLA RICE WITH CRAYFISH, LEMONGRASS AND ASPARAGUS

Serves 6
Preparation time: 50 minutes
Cooking time: 17 minutes

100 ml (scant ½ cup) olive oil

200 g (7 oz) spring onions (scallions), trimmed

100 g (3½ oz) garlic shoots, trimmed

2 cloves garlic, finely chopped

2 bunches green asparagus, trimmed and cut into fine strips

1 green bell pepper, seeded and cut into fine strips

3 large, ripe tomatoes, halved, seeded and grated, skin discarded

1 teaspoon Spanish sweet smoked paprika

600 g (3 cups) bomba or other short-grain rice

½ teaspoon saffron threads, toasted and pounded

salt and pepper

For the crayfish fumet

2 kg (4½ lb) large crayfish

100 ml (scant ½ cup) olive oil

1 carrot, cut into fine strips

2 celery stalks, finely chopped

1 onion, finely chopped

1 bouquet garni (garlic, rosemary, bay leaf, thyme)

Flavourings

1 lemongrass stalk, tough outer layers removed, bruised and sliced into thin rounds

finely grated zest of ¼ lime

10 g (¼ oz) fresh ginger, about 3 mm (⅛ inch) long, peeled and cut into very thin slices

For a moist texture, use a 60-cm (24-inch) paella pan.

Clean the crayfish. Pull the central tail flipper, twisting it slightly as you do so. The intestine can now be pulled out, attached to the flipper. Select and set aside the 6 largest crayfish whole, then separate the heads from the tails of the remaining crayfish and and set the tails aside. Put the flavourings – lemongrass, lime zest and ginger slices – into a muslin (cheesecloth) bouquet garni bag, and secure tightly.

Make the fumet. Heat the olive oil in the paella pan and sauté the reserved crayfish heads over very high heat. When they have browned, add the carrot, celery, onion and bouquet garni with herbs. Pour in sufficient water to cover, bring to a boil, add the bouquet garni bag of flavourings and cook for 20 minutes. Remove the pan from the heat. Carefully strain the fumet through a fine-mesh sieve; discard the solids. Measure 1.2 litres (5 cups) of the fumet and keep hot.

To make the paella, wash the paella pan and dry with paper towels. Make sure that the pan is completely level to ensure that the paella cooks evenly. Heat the olive oil in the pan over very high heat or position the pan as close as possible to the heat source. Sauté the 6 reserved crayfish and the crayfish tails, then remove and set aside. Sauté the spring onions (scallions), garlic shoots and cloves, asparagus and green bell pepper for a few minutes until softened but not browned; push these ingredients to the side of the pan. Cook the grated tomato, stirring, until reduced and thickened. Stir through the other ingredients in the pan until well mixed. Add the paprika and cook briefly for a few seconds more; take care not to burn. Pour in the hot fumet and bring to a boil over very high heat. Allow to boil for 2 minutes. Sprinkle in the rice, and then the saffron, spreading it out evenly in the paella pan. Return to a boil, taste and season with salt if needed.

Distribute all the ingredients evenly in the pan, then arrange the crayfish tails and the 6 whole crayfish in the centre. After 5 minutes, reduce the heat by removing some embers from under the pan or raising the trivet or grill rack so that the pan is further away from the heat source. When the rice starts to rise to the surface of the liquid, reduce the heat under the pan so that the liquid remains at a very gentle simmer.

Finish cooking the rice, allowing all the remaining fumet in the pan to evaporate. Taste to check whether the rice is cooked: it should be tender but still very slightly firm to the bite. If it is a little too firm, cover the paella with a clean, damp dish towel for 2–3 minutes to finish cooking. If it is much too firm, sprinkle a few tablespoons of very hot water over the surface of the rice and wait until the rice is tender. Remove from the heat and allow to rest for 3 minutes before serving.

PAELLA RICE WITH CHICKEN AND LANGOUSTINES

Serves 6
Preparation time: 40 minutes
Cooking time: 17 minutes

6 young, tender artichokes

2 limes

200 ml (scant 1 cup) olive oil

1×1.5-kg (3¼-lb) organic free-range chicken, boned and skin removed, cut into 35-g (1½-oz) pieces

8 langoustines, rinsed

2 cloves garlic, finely chopped

1 green bell pepper, seeded and cut into strips

200 g (7 oz) green beans, trimmed

6 spring onions (scallions)

500 g (1 lb 2 oz) squid, cleaned and prepared, cut into rings

1 medium–large tomato, halved, seeded and grated, skin discarded, or finely diced

1 teaspoon Spanish sweet smoked paprika

400 g (2 cups) bomba or other short-grain rice

1½ teaspoons saffron threads, toasted and pounded

salt and pepper

Flavourings

1 sprig of rosemary

2 sprigs of thyme

2 bay leaves

For a moist texture, use a 51-cm (20½-inch) paella pan.

Preheat the barbecue or grill. Trim the artichokes, remove the hairy chokes if necessary and peel the stalks if tough. Slice each artichoke into quarters, and rub all the cut surfaces with the freshly cut halves of 1 of the limes. Set aside in a bowl of cold water acidulated with lime juice. Put the herb flavourings (rosemary, thyme and bay leaves) into a muslin (cheesecloth) bouquet garni bag and secure tightly. Finely grate the zest of the second lime. Set aside.

Make sure that the paella pan is completely level to ensure that the paella is evenly cooked. Heat the olive oil in the pan over low heat, and gently sauté the chicken pieces without letting them brown too much (you will need to position the paella pan at the correct distance from the heat source). Push the chicken pieces towards the edge of the pan, and sauté the langoustines gently in the centre until half cooked. Remove the langoustines from the pan and keep warm to one side, covered with aluminium foil. Sauté the garlic gently in the centre of the pan, then add the vegetables. Gently sauté until starting to soften. Push the vegetables towards the edge of the pan, and gently sauté the squid rings in the centre until they are half cooked. Push these away to the side of the pan. Add the grated tomato to the centre of the pan, and cook over low heat until thickened and reduced.

Add the paprika and cook for a few seconds more. Pour in 1 litre (4¼ cups) water, bring to a boil and continue boiling for 1 minute over the hottest part of the barbecue or grill. Add the bouquet garni bag of herbs. Use a piece of aluminium foil folded over the lip of the pan to mark the level of the liquid. Add another 1 litre (4¼ cups) water and bring to a boil. Allow the liquid to evaporate until it reaches the point indicated by the marker (if the level of liquid falls below this, add more very hot water). Sprinkle in the rice, followed by the saffron, distributing it evenly all over the pan. Taste and season with salt if needed. Arrange the ingredients, including the langoustines, on top.

After 5 minutes, reduce the heat by removing some embers from under the pan or raising the trivet or grill rack so that the pan is further away from the heat source. Remove and discard the bag of herbs. When the rice starts to rise to the surface, reduce the heat so that it simmers very gently. Add the langoustines and finish cooking the rice, allowing all the remaining liquid in the pan to evaporate. Taste to check whether the rice is cooked: it should be tender, but still very slightly firm to the bite. If it is a little too firm, cover the paella with a clean, damp dish towel for 2–3 minutes to finish cooking. If it is much too firm, sprinkle a few tablespoons of hot water over the surface of the rice and continue cooking until the rice is tender. Allow to rest for 3 minutes before serving.

ARROZ EN PAELLA DE CAZA
PAELLA RICE WITH GAME

Serves 6
Preparation time: 50 minutes
Cooking time: 17 minutes

3 saddles of hare fillet, trimmed

3 saddles of wild rabbit fillet, trimmed

2 red-legged or other partridges, plucked and drawn (reserve the livers); breasts taken off the bone, thighs separated and boned (you can ask your game supplier to do this for you)

1 hare's liver

1 rabbit's liver

12 baby artichokes

1 lemon, halved

100 ml (scant ½ cup) extra-virgin olive oil

200 g (7 oz) baby turnips

200 g (7 oz) spring onions (scallions)

100 g (3½ oz) garlic shoots

4 blanched almonds

2 cloves garlic

1 ñora pepper, stalk removed and seeded, coarsely crumbled

1 sprig of flat-leaf parsley

1 green bell pepper, seeded and skinned

100 g (½ cup) large white haricot (navy) beans, cooked and drained

3 tomatoes, seeded and grated, skin discarded

1 teaspoon Spanish sweet smoked paprika

175 ml (¾ cup) dry red wine

4 tablespoons best-quality matured sherry vinegar

600 g (3 cups) bomba or other short-grain rice

1½ teaspoons saffron threads, toasted and pounded

salt and pepper

Spices and flavourings

1 teaspoon Sichuan peppercorns

1 teaspoon black peppercorns

1 teaspoon green peppercorns

1 teaspoon pink peppercorns

1 star anise

1 clove

1 sprig of rosemary

1 sprig of flat-leaf parsley

For a moist texture, use a 60-cm (24-inch) paella pan.

Preheat the barbecue or grill. Rinse all the pieces of game thoroughly to get rid of any traces of blood and bone splinters. Pat dry with a clean cloth or paper towels. Cut the partridge breasts away from the bone, and slice each breast fillet in half. Cut the thigh meat in half. Cut each saddle into four pieces. Rinse the livers and chop coarsely; season with salt and pepper and set aside. Trim the baby artichokes and peel the stalks if tough; slice them into quarters and rub the cut surfaces with a lemon half. Put in a bowl of water acidulated with lemon juice and set aside.

Toast all the dried spices lightly in a dry frying pan or skillet over medium-high heat until fragrant. Put into a muslin (cheesecloth) bouquet garni bag with the rosemary and parsley, and secure tightly.

Make sure that the paella pan is completely level to ensure that the paella cooks evenly. Heat the olive oil in the pan over medium-high (position the pan close to the heat source or over the hottest part of the barbecue of grill). Brown the pieces of game and liver lightly all over, beginning with the hare fillets. When these are golden brown, push to the edge of the pan and brown the pieces of partridge meat; push to the sides of the pan and repeat the process with the saddle of rabbit, ending with the livers. Remove the livers from the pan as soon as they have browned lightly (they should still be uncooked in the middle) and set aside.

Add the drained artichokes to the centre of the pan and sauté until starting to soften, followed by the turnips, spring onions (scallions) and garlic shoots in this order. Continue sautéing until all the vegetables have softened and lightly browned. Mix together before pushing them to the edge of the pan.

Add the almonds, garlic cloves, ñora pepper and parsley to the centre of the pan and gently sauté. Remove this mixture from the pan as soon as the almonds start to colour, and put in a mortar with the reserved livers. Set aside.

Add the bell pepper and haricot (navy) beans to pan, and sauté for a few minutes until it has softened and lightly browned. Push towards the edge of the pan and add the grated tomatoes to the centre. Cook, stirring, until thickened and reduced. Add the paprika and cook briefly for a few seconds more; take care not to burn. Mix together all the contents of the pan, and pour in the red wine. Deglaze the pan, scraping up any bits on the bottom with a wooden spatula. When the alcohol has almost completely evaporated, pour in the vinegar and cook until this has also evaporated, repeating the deglazing process.

Pour 1.2 litres (5 cups) water into the paella pan, and add the bouquet garni bag of spices and herbs. Use a piece of aluminium foil folded over the rim of the pan to mark the level of the liquid at this point.

Set the paella over very high heat by positioning the trivet or grill rack very close to the embers or turning up the heat if using a gas-fired barbecue or grill. Bring to a boil. Continue boiling for 1 minute, then add 300 ml (1½ cups) water. Bring to a boil once again. Continue boiling until the water has fallen to the level indicated by the aluminium foil marker. Carefully sprinkle in the rice and add the saffron, distributing it evenly all over the pan.

Using a pestle, pound the contents of the mortar to a smooth paste. Thin the paste with a few tablespoons of the hot liquid from the paella pan, then pour into the pan and stir through. Arrange the vegetables and pieces of game evenly over the entire pan; they cannot be moved from this point on because the rice needs to cook undisturbed.

After 5 minutes, taste and add salt if needed. Reduce the heat by removing some embers under the pan or by raising the trivet or grill rack so that the pan is further away from the heat source. Remove and discard the bag of spices and herbs. When the rice starts to rise to the surface, position the paella pan far enough away from the heat source that it boils very gently over low heat.

Finish cooking the rice, allowing all the remaining liquid in the pan to evaporate. Taste to check whether the rice is cooked: it should be tender but still very slightly firm to the bite. If it is a little too firm, place a clean, damp dish towel over the paella and leave for 2–3 minutes to finish cooking. If it is still much too firm, sprinkle a few tablespoons of hot water over the rice and continue cooking until the rice is tender.

'RETURN TO BUENOS AIRES' PAELLA RICE

Serves 6
Preparation time: 1 hour
Cooking time: 17 minutes

300 g (2½ cups) peeled and seeded pumpkin, cut into 2-cm (¾-inch) cubes

6 plum (roma) tomatoes

2 courgettes (zucchini), cut into 1-cm (½-inch) rounds

3 baby artichokes, rinsed, trimmed and cut into quarters lengthwise

2 sweet corn cobs, cut into 3-cm (1¼-inch) thick slices

2 morcilla sausages

2 smoked cooking chorizo (the larger, softer Galician variety)

1 set of calf's sweetbreads, cleaned and cut into 6 pieces

1 kg (2¼ lb) boned short ribs of beef

300 g (11 oz) chinchulines (beef chitterlings), thoroughly cleaned and cut into 20-cm (8-inch) lengths

200 ml (scant 1 cup) olive oil

6 cloves garlic

150 g (5 oz) green beans, trimmed

200 g (scant 1 cup) fresh tomato purée or passata (puréed canned tomatoes)

1 teaspoon smoked sweet paprika

2 tablespoons maté tea (in a teabag or infusing sachet)

600 g (3 cups) bomba or other short-grain rice

1 teaspoon saffron threads, toasted and pounded

1 small sprig of rosemary

salt and pepper

Vegetables and meats that have already been grilled on the barbecue or grill are called for here.

For a moist paella, use a 60-cm (24-inch) paella pan.

Before you start cooking the paella, preheat the barbecue or grill, and grill the vegetables (pumpkin, tomatoes, courgettes (zucchini), artichokes and sweet corn) and various meats and sausages. The vegetables should be grilled only until they start to soften and colour; otherwise they over-cook once added to the paella. The meats are cooked to your liking; they are served alongside the paella. As you finish grilling the different ingredients, set them aside to keep warm, covered with aluminium foil. Cut up the meats and sausages to provide 6 portions.

Make sure that the paella pan is completely level to ensure that the paella cooks evenly. Heat the oil in the paella pan over very high heat (position the pan very close to the heat source or over the hottest part of the barbecue or grill). Add the garlic and sauté until just starting to colour. Add the artichokes and green beans to the pan. Sauté for a few minutes until starting to brown, then add the tomato purée and other grilled vegetables. Stir well and cook until the tomato has thickened and reduced. Add the paprika and cook briefly for a few seconds more, taking care that it does not burn. Pour in 1.5 litres (6¼ cups) water immediately. Add the maté tea. Mark the level of the liquid at this point with a piece of aluminium foil folded over the rim of the pan. Pour 500 ml (2¼ cups) water into the pan and cook until the liquid has evaporated to the level indicated by the aluminium foil marker.

Sprinkle in all the rice and add the saffron, distributing the rice evenly all over the paella pan. Taste and season with salt if needed. Bring to a boil over very high heat (position the pan very close to the embers or over the hottest part of the barbecue). After 5 minutes, taste again and reduce the heat by removing some of the embers under the pan or adjusting the trivet or grill rack upwards (or by moving the pan to a cooler part of the barbecue or grill). Remove and discard the maté teabag or infusing sachet.

When the rice starts to rise to the surface of the liquid, position the paella pan as far away from the heat source as possible, but make sure that the liquid stays at a very gentle simmer. Finish cooking the rice, allowing all the liquid in the pan to evaporate. Taste to check whether the rice is cooked: it should be tender but still slightly firm to the bite. If it is a little too firm, cover the paella with a clean, damp dish towel for 2–3 minutes to finish cooking. If it is much too firm, sprinkle several tablespoons of hot water over the surface of the rice and cook until the rice is tender.

PAELLA RICE WITH HARE AND MUSHROOMS

Serves 6
Preparation time: 1 hour
Cooking time: 17 minutes

1×1.5-kg (3¼-lb) oven-ready hare, jointed and boned (reserve the liver), cut into 40-g (1½-oz) pieces (you can ask your butcher or game supplier to do this for you)

200 ml (scant 1 cup) extra virgin olive oil

2 cloves garlic

2 dried ñora peppers, stalk removed and seeded, coarsely crumbled

100 g (3½ oz) garlic shoots, cut into fine strips

200 g (7 oz) spring onions (scallions), cut into fine strips

1 green bell pepper, seeded and cut into fine strips

1 bay leaf

2 ripe tomatoes, halved, seeded and grated, skin discarded

1 teaspoon Spanish sweet smoked paprika

1½ teaspoons saffron threads, toasted and pounded

600 g (3 cups) bomba or other short-grain rice

1 kg (2¼ lb) wild mushrooms in season (such as girolles, fresh porcini or chanterelles), cleaned and trimmed thinly sliced

salt and pepper

Spices and flavourings

½ teaspoon cumin seeds

½ teaspoon caraway seeds

½ teaspoon coriander seeds

½ teaspoon dried oregano

For a moist texture, use a 60-cm (24-inch) paella pan.

Keep the liver separate, and rinse the hare meat thoroughly under cold, gently running water to get rid of any traces of blood and bone splinters. Pat the pieces dry with a clean cloth or paper towels. Now rinse the liver, the slice it into sections, following the natural lines of the lobes. Put both the hare meat and the liver in the refrigerator, covered with clingfilm (plastic wrap). These two steps can be done up to a day in advance.

Preheat the barbecue or grill. Toast the spices and flavourings lightly in a dry frying pan or skillet over medium-high heat until fragrant. Put into a muslin (cheesecloth) bouquet garni bag and tie securely. Heat 2.4 litres (10 cups) water; keep hot until needed.

Make sure that the paella pan is completely level to ensure that the paella cooks evenly. Heat the olive oil in the paella pan over gentle heat (you will need to position the pan a suitable distance away from the heat or over a cooler part of the barbecue or grill), and lightly brown the pieces of meat, followed by the liver, garlic and ñora peppers. As soon as the liver has browned, remove from the pan, together with the garlic and ñora peppers, and put all these in a mortar. Set aside.

Push the pieces of meat to the edge of the pan, and add the garlic shoots, spring onions (scallions), green pepper and bay leaf to the centre. Gently sauté until the green pepper and spring onions are starting to soften and colour. Add the grated tomatoes and cook, stirring, until they have thickened and reduced, and the vegetables are soft. Add the paprika, stir through and cook briefly for a few seconds more; take care not to burn it.

Pour 1.2 litres (5 cups) of the very hot water into the paella pan and bring to a boil. Boil fast over very high heat for 1 minute (reposition the pan so that it is very close to the heat source). Add the bouquet garni bag of spices and oregano.

Use a piece of aluminium foil, folded over the rim of the paella pan, to mark the level of the liquid at this point. Add the remaining hot water and bring to a boil once again. Continue boiling until the liquid has reduced to the level indicated by the aluminium foil marker. If the liquid reduces quickly and falls below the level of the marker, add extra boiling water.

Carefully sprinkle in the rice, distributing it evenly all over the pan, followed by the mushrooms and saffron. Spread out the contents of the pan so that they are evenly distributed. Bring to a boil over a very high heat (with the pan positioned as close as possible to the heat source). Taste and season with salt if needed.

Using a pestle, pound the liver, garlic and ñora peppers in the mortar to a smooth paste. Thin the paste with a little of the hot liquid from the paella pan, then pour into the pan and stir through. After 5 minutes, reduce the heat by repositioning some of the embers under the pan or adjusting the trivet or grill rack (or by moving the pan to a cooler part of the barbecue or grill). Remove and discard the bag. When the rice starts to come to the surface of the liquid, reposition the pan far enough away from the heat source to maintain a very gentle simmer.

Finish cooking the rice, allowing all the remaining liquid in the pan to evaporate. Taste to check whether the rice is cooked: it should be tender but still very slightly firm to the bite. If it is a little too firm, cover the paella with a clean, damp dish towel and leave it for 2–3 minutes to finish cooking. If the grains are much too firm, sprinkle a few tablespoons of hot water over the surface of the rice and continue cooking until the rice is tender. Remove the pan from the heat and allow to rest for 3 minutes before serving.

If you want to make a socarret, or crust on the bottom of the pan, remove the dish towel and place the pan directly on the embers or over the hottest part of the barbecue or grill for 2 minutes. A thin layer of rice will stick to the bottom of the pan; the texture will be crunchy, with no trace of bitterness. Remove the pan from the heat and serve immediately.

MAJORCAN 'DIRTY' PAELLA RICE

Serves 6
Preparation time: 40 minutes
Cooking time: 17 minutes

200 ml (scant 1 cup) olive oil

6 cloves garlic

3 sprigs of flat-leaf parsley

400 g (14 oz) rabbit, on the bone (reserve the liver), chopped into 30-g (1-oz) pieces (you can ask your butcher to do this for you)

400 g (14 oz) chicken, on the bone and with skin on (reserve the liver), chopped into 30-g (1-oz) pieces

2 young pigeons or squab, on the bone (reserve the livers), chopped into 30-g (1-oz) pieces

400 g (14 oz) pork spare ribs, chopped into 30-g (1-oz) pieces

150 g (5 oz) snails, purged and cooked, shells discarded

150 g (5 oz) green beans, trimmed

3 very young artichokes, trimmed, stems peeled if tough and cut into quarters lengthwise

50 g (⅓ cup) fresh shelled green peas

1 red bell pepper, seeded and cut into fine strips

2 onions, finely chopped

50 g (2 oz) wild mushrooms (traditionally oyster mushrooms), trimmed and cleaned

200 g (7 oz) ripe tomatoes, halved, seeded and grated

1 teaspoon Spanish sweet smoked paprika

600 g (3 cups) bomba or other short-grain rice

1 teaspoon saffron threads, toasted and pounded

200 g (7 oz) best-quality matured sobrasada (Majorcan cured pork sausage), cut into small pieces

salt and pepper

Spices

1 cinnamon stick

15 cumin seeds

10 black peppercorns

1 nutmeg

This is a traditional Majorcan speciality. The description brut, *meaning 'dirty', refers both to the colour of the stock and the presence of bones in the paella. It should be eaten with good friends – you cannot avoid getting your hands dirty because the meat and poultry are still on the bone.*

For a moist texture, use a 60-cm (24-inch) paella pan.

Preheat the barbecue or grill. Put the spices in a muslin (cheese-cloth) bouquet garni bag and tie securely. Make sure that the paella pan is completely level to ensure the paella cooks evenly. Heat the olive oil in the pan over very high heat (position the pan close to the heat source). Briefly sauté the garlic, parsley and chicken, rabbit and pigeon livers until lightly browned; do not allow the livers to cook through. Remove from the pan and place in a food processor. Set aside.

Over moderate heat, sauté the rabbit, poultry, pork and snails until half cooked. Add the beans, artichokes, peas, bell pepper, onions and mushrooms, and continue sautéing until the vegetables have browned. Push to the edge of the pan and add the grated tomatoes to the centre. Cook, stirring, until the tomatoes have thickened and reduced. Add the paprika and cook briefly for a few seconds more, taking care it does not burn. Pour in 1.5 litres (6 ⅓ cups) water, then add the bouquet garni bag of spices. Make up the liquid that has evaporated by adding 500 ml (2¼ cups) water. Quickly process the reserved livers with a little hot stock from the pan; pour this mixture into the pan. Stir until well mixed.

Sprinkle in the rice, distributing it evenly all over the pan, then add the saffron. Taste and add salt if needed. Arrange all the ingredients evenly and attractively in the pan: they will stay put until they are served (the rice must be left to cook undisturbed from now onwards). Bring to a boil once again over very high heat, then add the pieces of sobrasada. Remove and discard the bag containing the spices. After 5 minutes taste again. Reduce the heat by removing some of the embers under the paella pan or raising the trivet or grill rack.

When the rice starts to rise to the surface of the liquid, position the pan as far away from the heat as possible to maintain a very gentle simmer. Finish cooking the rice, allowing all the remaining liquid in the pan to evaporate. Taste the rice to check whether it is cooked: it should be tender but still slightly firm to the bite. If the rice is little too firm, cover the paella with a clean, damp dish towel for 2–3 minutes to finish cooking. If it is much too firm, sprinkle a few tablespoons of very hot water over the surface of the rice and cook until the rice is tender. It should be moist, but not excessively so. Serve immediately.

PAELLAS WITHOUT RICE

WHY PAELLAS WITHOUT RICE?

The following recipes, although cooked in a paella pan, are made without rice. The name for these dishes is *fideuá*, a term which is derived from the Catalan *fideu* (*fideo* in Spanish), a vermicelli-like noodle. Traditionally, dried noodles of different sizes are used, either hollow or solid, usually curved, rather thin and 1–2 cm (½–1 inch) long. Before adding them to a dish, you can either fry the noodles in plenty of oil or cook them in the oven. You can also combine the two techniques: deep- or pan-fry half of them and cook the other half in the oven, then mix the two types of noodles together. In both cases you must use enough oil to ensure that the noodles brown evenly.

It is clear that the Spanish methods of preparing pasta and paella rice (two techniques that are actually Mediterranean in origin) are historically connected and have developed along parallel lines. This type of dish may have evolved in response to a scarcity of cereals, such as rice, due to drought, which made cooks resort to substitute ingredients. Or perhaps it came about through negligence (the cook having one day forgotten to buy the rice) or quite simply as a result of gastronomic curiosity. Theories on the origin of *fideuá* abound, but what interests me most of all is the possibility of preparing paella with pasta, an ingredient that plays a role so similar to rice in our diets that it can virtually be used as a substitute.

This is why I have come up with a few paellas containing less obvious ingredients. As with rice and pasta, these are intended to emphasize the flavour of the other ingredients in the dish. They should be cooked until just tender but still firm to the bite – they must not be at all mushy or gluey.

FIDEUÁ DE MARISCO
FIDEUÁ WITH SEAFOOD

Serves 2
Preparation: 30 minutes
(excluding fumet)
Cooking time: 9 minutes

For the picada

1 clove garlic

50 ml (¼ cup) olive oil

3 whole almonds

1 dried ñora pepper, stalk removed and seeded, coarsely crumbled

2 sprigs of flat-leaf parsley

For the fideuá

400 ml (1¾ cups) Rock Fish Fumet (page 49)

100 ml (scant ½ cup) olive oil

2 langoustines, heads removed and reserved

6 uncooked king prawns (jumbo shrimp), heads removed and reserved

50 g (2 oz) squid, cleaned and prepared, cut into large dice

100 g (3½ oz) monkfish fillet, cut into pieces

200 g (7 oz) coquillettes (small elbow macaroni)

200 ml (scant 1 cup) Seafood Stock for Fideuá (page 42)

1 teaspoon Spanish sweet smoked paprika

1 teaspoon saffron threads, toasted and pounded

lime

salt

You can cook the pasta used here in a paella pan, as specified in this recipe, or pan-fry it separately in a frying pan or skillet. With the latter you have more control over how well browned and crispy the pasta becomes. You can also add it to the paella pan after the fumet has come to a boil. This method is a little riskier because it means you have to be precise as to exactly how much fumet will be needed to cook the pasta, which is lighter in texture when cooked this way. The lime zest grated directly onto the stock imparts its aroma to the dish and marries well with the other ingredients. By using lime you avoid the slight acidity that lemon juice inevitably adds when poured directly onto pasta.

For a moist texture, use a 30-cm (12-inch) paella pan suitable for use on the stove and in the oven.

First, make the picada. Heat the olive oil in a small pan and gently sauté the garlic, almonds, ñora pepper and parsley until they release their aroma and are lightly browned. Put the ingredients into a mortar and pound them with the garlic to a paste with a pestle, or blend to a paste in a food processor. Set the picada aside.

Preheat the oven to 150°C/300°F/Gas Mark 2, and heat the Rock Fish Fumet; do not allow it to boil. Heat the olive oil in a paella pan over low heat, and add the langoustine and king prawn (jumbo shrimp) heads, squid and monkfish. Gently sauté, stirring well, until starting to brown. Remove the langoustines and king prawn heads from the pan and set aside. Add the pasta to the pan and pan-fry gently until lightly and evenly browned, taking care that they do not burn. Add the picada and pour in the Seafood Stock for Fideuá. Mix everything together with a wooden spatula. Add the paprika and cook for a few seconds, taking care that it does not burn.

Pour the hot Rock Fish Fumet into the pan, add the saffron and finely grate the lime zest all over the top. Bring to a boil and, if you have a timer, set it to 9 minutes. After 5 minutes, the noodles should rise to the surface. Taste the fumet and season with salt, bearing in mind that the flavours will become more pronounced as the liquid evaporates. Quickly arrange the langoustine and king prawn tails evenly on top of the noodles, and carefully transfer the paella pan to the preheated oven for 4 minutes.

Remove the paella pan from the oven. If any liquid is left, reduce over high heat on top of the stove. Allow the paella to rest for 2 minutes, then serve in the centre of the table.

FIDEO NOODLES WITH SQUID

Serves 2
Preparation time: 25 minutes
(excluding fumet)
Cooking time: 14 minutes

300 g (11 oz) fideo noodles or other
very fine noodles, such as vermicelli,
broken into short lengths

vegetable oil for deep-frying

500 ml (2¼ cups) Fish Fumet (page 48)

50 ml (¼ cup) Garlic Oil (page 60)

200 g (7 oz) squid, cleaned and
prepared, cut into very small dice

2 spring onions (scallions), cut into
fine strips

½ teaspoon Spanish sweet
smoked paprika

100 ml (scant ½ cup) fumet for
Paella Rice 'a Banda' (page 68)

¼ teaspoon saffron threads, toasted
and pounded

salt

Before beginning to make this classic Catalan recipe, you need to deep-fry the fine noodles in plenty of oil. You can also cook them in the oven, or mix the two methods – a trick I was taught by the chef at the Via Veneto restaurant in Barcelona one memorable evening. This dish can also be made in an earthenware dish, but a paella pan is ideal because it enables you to control the texture of the noodles. One curious detail is the appearance of the noodles after their final cooking in the oven – they puff up in the pan. They are mixed through once the dish is at the table. The finished dish should be quite liquid – all'onda, or 'wavy', as the Italians describe certain risottos.

For a moist texture, use a 40-cm (16-inch) paella pan suitable for use on the stove and in the oven.

First, deep-fry half the noodles. Heat enough oil for deep-frying in a deep, heavy frying pan or skillet to 150°C/300°F. Carefully plunge half the noodles into the hot oil. Deep-fry until evenly browned. Lift the noodles out of the pan with a metal slotted spoon. Drain in a sieve or metal colander, then spread out on a plate lined with paper towels. Set aside. Preheat the oven to 150°C/300°F/Gas Mark 2.

Bake the remaining noodles in an ovenproof dish for 6 minutes. Remove them from the oven and add them to the fried noodles.

Heat the Fish Fumet but do not allow it to boil. Put the Garlic Oil in a paella pan over low heat, and gently sauté the squid and spring onions until all the juices have evaporated. Add the fumet for Paella Rice 'a Banda'. Stir well, then add the paprika, followed by the deep-fried and roasted noodles. Mix again, then add the hot Fish Fumet. Bring to a boil and, if you have a timer, set it to 14 minutes.

Sprinkle in the saffron, and boil rapidly for 3 minutes. Taste the liquid and season with salt, bearing in mind that the flavours will become more pronounced as the liquid evaporates. Carefully transfer to the oven for 11 minutes. Remove the pan from the oven and serve immediately.

QUINOA PAELLA WITH SPRING VEGETABLES

Serves 2
Preparation time: 20 minutes
(excluding stock)
Cooking time: 17 minutes

2 small carrots

2 small turnips

10 fresh asparagus spears, trimmed

50 g (⅓ cup) fresh broad (fava) beans, shelled

2 very young, fresh artichokes

1 lemon, halved

450 ml (scant 2 cups) Vegetable Stock (page 38)

50 ml (¼ cup) olive oil

200 g (2 cups) spring onions (scallions), cut into fine strips

1 clove garlic, finely chopped

200 g (scant 1¼ cups) quinoa

200 g (scant 1 cup) Tomato Sofrito (page 54) or passata (puréed canned tomatoes)

½ teaspoon Spanish sweet smoked paprika

¼ teaspoon saffron threads, toasted and pounded

salt

For a moist texture, use a 34-cm (13½-inch) paella pan suitable for use on the stove and in the oven.

Wash the carrots and turnips, and pat dry in a clean cloth or with paper towels. Cut the stalks off the asparagus. Keep 7 of the asparagus tips whole. Chop the remaining 3 tips into very fine rounds, then set aside in iced water. Blanch the broad (fava) beans in boiling water for 5 seconds, then immediately refresh under cold water; drain. Peel off the remaining tough skins (they should slip off easily). Trim the artichokes, removing any tough outer leaves (if the artichokes are young and tender, you will not need to worry about removing the hairy choke). Rub them all over with the cut lemon to prevent oxidation and discoloration. Set aside in water acidulated with lemon juice.

Next, preheat the oven to 150°C/300°F/Gas Mark 2, and heat the Vegetable Stock, but do not allow it to boil.

Heat the olive oil in a paella pan over medium heat, and sauté the carrots, turnips, broad (fava) beans, asparagus (except the chopped tips), artichokes and spring onions for 2 minutes. Add the garlic to the centre of the pan and continue cooking until the vegetables are softened and lightly browned.

Add the quinoa and sauté until translucent, without allowing it to burn, just as if it were rice for a paella. Add the sofrito or passata, and stir with a wooden spatula, scraping the bottom of the paella pan thoroughly. Allow to thicken, then add the paprika. Cook for a few seconds more, taking care that it does not burn. Pour in the hot Vegetable Stock, stir and bring to a boil. Add the saffron and continue to cook over very high heat. If you have a timer, set to 17 minutes.

After 5 minutes, the quinoa rises to the surface. Taste the stock and add a little salt if needed, bearing in mind that the seasonings and flavours will become more pronounced as the liquid reduces.

Carefully transfer the paella pan to the oven for 12 minutes. Remove the paella pan from the oven and allow to rest for 3 minutes. Meanwhile, thoroughly drain the chopped asparagus tips, pat dry with paper towels and sprinkle all over the paella. Serve immediately.

VERMICELLI PAELLA WITH FISH AND SEAFOOD

Serves 3
Preparation time: 40 minutes
(excluding stock)
Cooking time: 9 minutes

For the sofrito

50 ml (¼ cup) olive oil

½ leek, finely sliced

½ carrot, finely sliced into strips

½ onion, finely chopped

2 cloves garlic, finely chopped

4 prawns (shrimp)

2 cooked whole swimming crabs or shore (green) crabs, cleaned

2 hazelnuts

2 almonds

1 dried ñora pepper, stalk removed and seeded, coarsely crumbled

2–3 medium fresh tomatoes, halved, seeded and grated, skins discarded

For the fideo noodles

vegetable oil for deep-frying

200 g (7 oz) fideo noodles or similar thin noodles such as vermicelli, broken into short lengths

12 fresh clams, cleaned and scrubbed

400 ml (1¾ cups) Seafood Stock for Fideuá (page 42)

100 ml (scant ½ cup) olive oil

80 g (2¾ oz) small squid, cleaned and prepared, well drained

1 teaspoon Spanish sweet smoked paprika

4 king prawns (jumbo shrimp), peeled and deveined (reserve the heads)

2 cooked langoustine tails, peeled

2 red mullet, cleaned and filleted

¼ teaspoon saffron threads, toasted and pounded

salt

For a moist texture, use a 34-cm (13½-inch) paella pan suitable for use on the stove and in the oven.

For this dish, the noodles must be fried in advance. Heat enough oil for deep-frying in a deep, heavy frying pan or skillet to 150°C/300°F. Carefully plunge the noodles into the hot oil. Deep-fry until evenly browned. Lift the noodles out of the pan with a metal slotted spoon. Drain in a sieve or metal colander, then spread out on a plate lined with paper towels. Set aside.

Tap the clams on a work surface, and discard any that do not close tightly. Bring a large pan of water to a boil and plunge in the clams for 30 seconds. Drain the pan and set aside the clams, discarding any that have not opened.

To make the sofrito, heat the olive oil in the same pan over low heat, and gently sauté the vegetables and garlic until starting to soften. Add the prawns (shrimp), crabs, hazelnuts, almonds and ñora pepper, and cook for a few more minutes until lightly browned. Add the reserved prawn heads. Cook for a few minutes, then add the tomatoes, scraping up any bits on the bottom of the pan with a wooden spatula. Allow to thicken and reduce for 10–12 minutes, then stir thoroughly. Push the mixture through a fine-mesh sieve, pressing down hard on the contents in order to yield as much sofrito as possible; discard the solids. You should end up with about 150 g (5 oz). Set aside.

Before making the paella, heat the stock gently but do not allow it to boil. Preheat the oven to 150°C/300°F/Gas Mark 2. Heat the olive oil in a paella pan over low heat, and add the squid. Sauté gently until all their juices have evaporated, then add the sofrito. Allow to reduce slightly, then sprinkle in the paprika. Cook for a few seconds, before pouring in the hot stock. Bring to a boil, and add the fried noodles and saffron. If you have a timer, set to 9 minutes. Reduce the heat and cook for 5 minutes.

Taste the stock and season with salt, bearing in mind that the flavours will become more pronounced as the liquid evaporates. Continue to cook for 4 minutes.

Carefully transfer the paella pan to the preheated oven and bake for 4 minutes. Remove the pan from the oven and quickly arrange the king prawns (jumbo shrimp), langoustines, clams and mullet fillets on top. Put the pan back in the oven for 3 minutes to cook the fish and thoroughly heat through the seafood. Serve immediately.

BLACK SPAGHETTI WITH HORN-OF-PLENTY MUSHROOMS

Serves 2
Preparation time: 35 minutes
(excluding fumet and stock)
Cooking time: 17 minutes

vegetable oil for deep-frying

300 g (11 oz) black spaghetti or
noodles, broken into short lengths

800 ml (3½ cups) Fish Fumet (page 48)

50 ml (¼ cup) olive oil

200 g (7 oz) baby cuttlefish, cleaned
and prepared, thinly sliced

100 g (3½ oz) horn-of-plenty
mushrooms, carefully cleaned

150 ml (⅔ cup) Black Stock (page 45)

1 teaspoon Spanish sweet
smoked paprika

3 spring onions (scallions), green part
only, thinly sliced into rings

salt

I suggest serving this paella with a rocket (arugula) salad. For a moist texture, use a 34-cm (13½-inch) paella pan suitable for use on the stove and in the oven.

First, deep-fry the spaghetti or noodles. Heat enough oil for deep-frying in a deep, heavy frying pan or skillet to 150°C/300°F. Carefully plunge the noodles into the hot oil. Deep-fry until evenly browned. Lift the noodles out of the pan with a metal slotted spoon. Drain in a sieve or metal colander, then spread out on a plate lined with paper towels. Set aside.

Next, preheat the oven to 150°C/300°F/Gas Mark 2, and heat the Fish Fumet but do not allow it to boil.

Heat the olive oil in a paella pan. Add the baby cuttlefish and horn-of-plenty mushrooms, and sauté until all the liquid has evaporated. Pour in the Black Stock, add the paprika and stir well. Add the spaghetti or noodles, mixing them well into the other ingredients, then pour in the hot Fish Fumet. Bring to a boil and, if you have a timer, set it to 17 minutes.

After 5 minutes, reduce the heat to as low as possible. Taste and season with salt, if needed, bearing in mind that the seasonings and flavours will become more pronounced as the liquid evaporates.

Carefully transfer the paella pan to the preheated oven and bake for 12 minutes. Remove the paella from the oven. Sprinkle with the spring onions (scallions) and serve immediately.

BOULGOUR EN PAELLA DE CHIPIRONES, CHANTARELLES, RAPE Y VERDURAS EN PAELLA
BULGUR-WHEAT PAELLA WITH SQUID, CHANTERELLES, MONKFISH AND VEGETABLES

Serves 2
Preparation time: 25 minutes
(excluding fumet)
Cooking time: 17 minutes

8 whole fresh squid, cleaned

400 ml (1¾ cups) Fish Fumet (page 48)

50 ml (¼ cup) olive oil

200 g (7 oz) monkfish tail, cut into
small cubes

200 g (2 cups) spring onions
(scallions), cut into fine strips

50 g (½ cup) turnip, cut into dice

4 whole baby carrots

50 g (½ cup) courgette (zucchini),
diced

50 g (½ cup) winter squash or
pumpkin, diced

100 g (3½ oz) small chanterelle
mushrooms, cleaned and trimmed

1 clove garlic, finely chopped

200 g (scant 1 cup) bulgur wheat

200 g (scant 1 cup) Tomato Sofrito
(page 54) or passata (puréed
canned tomatoes)

½ teaspoon Spanish sweet
smoked paprika

¼ teaspoon saffron threads, toasted
and pounded

½ celery stalk, finely sliced on the
diagonal

salt

For a moist texture use a 34-cm (13½-inch) paella pan suitable for use on the stove and in the oven.

Rinse the squid thoroughly and pat dry with paper towels. Use the tentacles and other edible parts to stuff the white mantle, or 'body', which is the main part of the squid. Fold the top edges of the stuffed squid 'pouches' over, and secure with a cocktail stick or toothpick. Set aside.

Next, preheat the oven to 150°C/300°F/Gas Mark 2, and heat the Fish Fumet but do not allow it to boil. Heat the olive oil in the paella pan, and sauté the squid over medium heat. When the squid are half cooked, add the monkfish and continue to sauté over medium heat until all the juices have evaporated. Add all the vegetables (except the celery) and the chanterelle mushrooms. Sauté over medium heat for 2 minutes, then remove the squid and monkfish from the pan. Set aside in a deep dish covered with a sheet of aluminium foil.

Put the garlic in the centre of the pan, surrounded by the remaining pan ingredients, and sauté gently. When all the ingredients are softened and lightly browned, add the bulgur wheat and sauté, without allowing to burn, until thoroughly coated and turning translucent. Pour in the sofrito or passata, and mix together all the ingredients well, scraping up any bits on the bottom of the pan with a wooden spatula. Add the paprika and cook for a few seconds, taking care that it does not burn. Pour in the hot Fish Fumet, stir and bring to a boil. Add the saffron. If you have a timer, set it to 17 minutes and continue cooking over medium heat for 5 minutes, until the bulgur wheat rises to the surface. Taste the liquid and season with salt, bearing in mind that the flavours will become more pronounced as the liquid evaporates.

Quickly arrange the reserved squid and monkfish evenly on top of the bulgur wheat, and carefully transfer the paella pan to the preheated oven for 12 minutes. Remove the paella from the oven and allow to rest for 3 minutes. Sprinkle the celery over the paella and serve immediately.

BARLEY PAELLA WITH SAUSAGES AND CHICKEN DUMPLINGS

Serves 2
Preparation time: 40 minutes +
12 hours for soaking
Cooking time: 2 hours for the stock,
17 minutes for the paella

For the pork and cabbage stock

1 salt-cured pig's trotter (foot)

20 g (2 tablespoons) chickpeas

400 g (14 oz) brine-salted ham bone
(or a ham knuckle)

½ stewing chicken

250 g (9 oz) pork neck

2 celery stalks

1 onion, studded with 1 clove

1 bay leaf

1 potato

1 carrot

200 g (2 cups) shredded Savoy cabbage

For the chicken dumplings

150 g (5 oz) skinless chicken fillets

½ onion

1 tablespoon chopped flat-leaf parsley

25 g (½ cup) fresh white breadcrumbs,
soaked in milk and drained

1 egg

25 g (¼ cup) plain (all-purpose) flour

100 ml (scant ½ cup) olive oil

salt

For the paella

600 ml (scant 2½ cups) pork and
cabbage stock (see above)

50 ml (¼ cup) olive oil

100 g (1½ cups) Savoy cabbage, cut
into 1-cm (½-inch) strips

2 cloves garlic, halved and crushed

200 g (1 cup) quick-cook barley

150 g (scant ¾ cup) Tomato Sofrito
(page 54) or passata (puréed
canned tomatoes)

½ teaspoon Spanish sweet
smoked paprika

2 boudin blanc or other white sausage

¼ teaspoon saffron threads, toasted
and pounded

50 g (2 oz) bacon

50 g (2 oz) cooking chorizo

salt

For a moist texture, use a 34-cm (13½-inch) paella pan suitable for use on the stove and in the oven.

The day before preparing the stock, put the pig's trotter (foot) in a bowl and fill with cold water to remove most of the salt. Soak the chickpeas in a separate bowl of cold water. The following day put all the stock ingredients (except the chickpeas) in a large casserole, heavy pan or Dutch oven. Fill with cold water to cover. Bring to a boil and skim off any scum that rises to the surface. Drain the soaked chickpeas and add to the stock. Reduce the heat and simmer gently for about 2 hours until the chickpeas are tender. Strain the stock through a fine-mesh sieve and set aside. Reserve the chickpeas and discard the other solids.

Make the chicken dumplings. Chop the chicken and onion very finely. Add the parsley, breadcrumbs and egg. Season with salt and mix with a metal spoon until evenly combined. Shape the mixture into 16 balls each about 2 cm (1 inch) in diameter. Coat in the flour, gently shaking off any excess. Heat the oil in a frying pan or skillet over medium heat, and sauté the dumplings until lightly browned all over. Drain and set aside.

Shortly before making the paella, preheat the oven to 150°C/300°F/Gas Mark 2 and heat 600 ml (2½ cups) pork and cabbage stock (reserve the remaining stock for reheating the meats). Do not allow it to boil.

Heat the olive oil in a paella pan and sauté the cabbage over medium heat until softened and starting to colour. Push to one side, add the garlic to the centre of the pan and continue sautéing gently for a minute or so. Add the barley and sauté, stirring continuously, until thoroughly coated and translucent; do not allow to catch and burn. Pour in the sofrito or passata and stir well, scraping up any bits on the bottom of the pan with a wooden spatula. Add the paprika and cook for a few seconds, taking care that it does not burn.

Pour the hot stock into the pan and add the reserved chickpeas. Stir and bring to a boil. Add the reserved chicken dumplings and boudin blanc, followed by the saffron. If you have a timer, set it to 17 minutes. Increase the heat to high and cook for 5 minutes, until the barley rises to the surface. Taste and season with salt, bearing in mind that the flavour will become more pronounced as the liquid evaporates.

Transfer the pan to the oven and cook for 12 minutes. Remove from the oven and allow to rest for 3 minutes before serving.

PAELLA WITH BEAN SPROUTS AND BOTTARGA

Serves 2
Preparation time: 15 minutes
(excluding stock)
Cooking time: 10 minutes

50 ml (¼ cup) olive oil

1×200-g (7-oz) cuttlefish, cleaned and cut into dice

700 g (1½ lb) bean sprouts, rinsed, drained and cut into pieces about 1 cm (½ inch) long

150 ml (⅔ cup) Prawn (Shrimp) and Red Mullet Stock (page 44)

pinch of Spanish sweet smoked paprika

¼ teaspoon saffron threads, toasted and pounded

50 g (2 oz) bottarga (dried, salted grey mullet roe)

salt

For a moist texture, use a 34-cm (13½-inch) paella pan suitable for use on the stove and in the oven.

Preheat the oven to 150°C/300°F/Gas Mark 2. Heat the olive oil in the paella pan and sauté the cuttlefish until it is starting to brown and any liquid has evaporated. Add the bean sprouts to the pan. Sauté lightly, stirring continuously, for 2 minutes. Pour in the stock and stir through well. Add the paprika and cook for a few seconds, taking care that it does not burn. Sprinkle in the saffron and stir through again until well combined. Cook over very high heat for 2 minutes.

Taste and season with salt if needed. If you have a timer, set it to 5 minutes. Carefully transfer the paella pan to the preheated oven for 4 minutes.

Remove the paella from the oven and continue cooking on the stove over very high heat for 1 minute to caramelize the bottom of the paella and form a *socarret* (crust).

Finely grate the bottarga directly onto the bean sprouts. Allow the paella to rest for 3 minutes, then serve.

'RETURN TO MARRAKECH' BARLEY PAELLA

Serves 2
Preparation time: 25 minutes
(excluding stock)
Cooking time: 17 minutes

vegetable oil, for deep-frying

3 tablespoons coriander (cilantro)
leaves

400 ml (1¾ cups) Chicken or Rabbit
Stock (page 51)

50 ml (¼ cup) olive oil

4 fairly spicy Merguez sausages, cut
into 2-cm (1-inch) dice

50 g (½ cup) courgette (zucchini),
thickly sliced into rounds

50 g (½ cup) carrot, thickly sliced
into rounds

50 g (½ cup) turnip, thickly sliced

50 g (⅓ cup) drained cooked
chickpeas

2 cloves garlic, halved and
finely chopped

200 g (1½ cups) dried, cracked
barley or bulgur wheat

150 g (scant ¾ cup) Tomato Sofrito
(page 54) or passata (puréed
canned tomatoes)

1 teaspoon ras el hanout

½ teaspoon ground cumin

4 pitted dried dates

1 tablespoon currants

¼ teaspoon saffron threads, toasted
and pounded

3–4 tablespoons harissa, to serve

If you are really fond of hot, spicy flavours, you can replace the sofrito with harissa. For a moist texture, use a 34-cm (13½-inch) paella pan suitable for use on the stove and in the oven.

Heat the vegetable oil for deep-frying in a heavy frying pan or skillet, and drop in the coriander (cilantro) leaves. Deep-fry until crisp, taking care not to burn them. Using a slotted spoon, lift them carefully out of the pan and set aside on a plate lined with paper towels, taking care not to break them.

To make the paella, preheat the oven to 150°C/300°F/Gas Mark 2 and heat the stock; do not allow it to boil. Heat the olive oil in the paella pan and pan-fry the sausages over medium heat for a few minutes until browned. Push slightly to one side, and add the courgette (zucchini), carrot, turnip, chickpeas and garlic to the centre of the pan. Sauté until the vegetables are softened and lightly browned, then add the barley or bulgur wheat, stirring continuously to prevent it from catching and burning, and cook until the grains are thoroughly coated and translucent. Add the sofrito or passata and stir with a wooden spatula, scraping up any bits on the bottom of the pan. Allow to thicken, then sprinkle in the ras el hanout and cumin. Cook for a little longer, stirring, taking care that the spices do not burn.

Pour the hot stock into the pan, then add the dates and currants. Stir and bring to a boil. Add the saffron, stir through once again and continue to cook over very high heat. If you have a timer, set it to 17 minutes.

After 5 minutes, the barley should rise to the surface of the liquid. Taste the stock and season with salt, bearing in mind that the flavours will become more pronounced as the liquid evaporates.

Carefully transfer the paella pan to the preheated oven and bake for 12 minutes. Remove from the oven and allow the paella to rest for 3 minutes. Sprinkle the deep-fried coriander leaves on top and serve the paella in the pan, accompanied by a small bowl of harissa.

SWEET PAELLAS

PAELLAS IN THE WORLD OF DESSERTS

It was the work of French pastry chef Pierre Hermé – his light confections served in little porcelain dishes, to be eaten with a spoon while sitting companionably around the table – that brought back many childhood memories and first gave me the idea of adapting paella techniques for desserts.

All these sweet dishes should be cooked in stainless steel or enamelled paella pans to avoid oxidation. They are cold desserts and can be made one or two days in advance. Their preparation is not just a question of making paella with rice and milk. The aim is to create a very special flavour with different ingredients, and, as with savoury paellas, the rice functions as the vehicle for the highly individual taste of each ingredient. The steps to be followed when making sweet paella do not closely resemble those set out in the recipes for the savoury paellas: desserts call for a different culinary procedure.

Fresh fruit, sweet fruit sauces, cooked dried fruit or compotes, sorbets, ice creams – all these are wonderful accompaniments for these dishes. It is also an excellent idea to serve them with a dessert wine, a liqueur, Champagne or even a fruit-flavoured eau de vie.

SWEET PAELLA RICE WITH PEARS IN WHITE WINE

Serves 6
Preparation time: 20 minutes
Cooking time: 45 minutes

1 vanilla bean

1 lemon

1 orange

1 litre (4¼ cups) Moscatel sweet white wine

2 cinnamon sticks

1 star anise

4 ripe Williams (Bartlett) pears

200 g (1 cup) short-grain pudding (pearl) rice

50 g (¼ cup) caster (superfine) sugar, plus extra, to taste

2½ tablespoons runny honey

1½ teaspoons raisins

10 pitted ready-to-eat prunes

vanilla ice cream, to serve

A sweet dessert wine goes well with this, especially a fortified Mistela wine from Tarragona wine region in Catalonia. Use a 33-cm (13-inch) stainless steel or enamelled paella pan.

Peel and core the pears, and cut into 8 equal segments. Slit the vanilla bean lengthwise and use the tip of a sharp knife to scrape out the seeds; set both of these aside. Use a vegetable peeler to remove the zest of the lemon and the orange, leaving all the white pith behind. Pour the Moscatel wine into a paella pan and add 400 ml (1¾ cups) water. Add the vanilla bean and seeds, orange and lemon zests, cinnamon and star anise. Bring to a boil.

Add the rice to the paella pan, spreading it evenly over the bottom, then add the pears. Reduce the heat to very low and cook for 45 minutes.

After about 20 minutes, add the sugar and honey. Stir well until the sugar has dissolved, then add the raisins and prunes. Taste and add a little extra sugar if desired. Remove and discard the citrus zest, cinnamon sticks and vanilla bean. Distribute the remaining items, evenly spaced, among the rice.

When the rice is cooked, remove the pan from the heat and allow to cool at room temperature. Once the rice has cooled completely, cover with clingfilm (plastic wrap), making sure it is in direct contact with the entire surface of the rice. Transfer to the refrigerator and chill until just before serving. Serve with a scoop of vanilla ice cream placed next to the rice and pears.

SWEET PAELLA RICE WITH STRAWBERRIES, ALMONDS AND ROSEMARY

Serves 6
Preparation time: 30 minutes
Cooking time: 45 minutes

1 vanilla bean

1 lemon

1 orange

25 g (scant 1 cup) tender, young rosemary leaves

1 cinnamon stick

½ teaspoon whole black peppercorns

25 g (1 oz) raw, freshly gathered and shelled almonds (see note)

1.4 litres (6 cups) full-fat (whole) milk

175 g (scant 1 cup) short-grain pudding (pearl) rice

1 bitter almond (or 1 teaspoon pure almond extract; see note)

100 g (½ cup) caster (superfine) sugar

250 g (1¾ cups) ripe, firm strawberries, rinsed and hulled

A glass of pink Champagne is the ideal accompaniment for this paella. Fresh, raw (unpasteurized) sweet almonds and bitter almonds can be difficult to find. Substitute best-quality organic unpeeled almonds and pure almond extract.

Use a 34-cm (13½-inch) stainless steel or enamelled paella pan.

Using a vegetable peeler, peel the zest from the lemon and orange, leaving all the white pith behind. Split the vanilla bean open along its length and scrape out the seeds with the tip of a sharp knife (reserve the seeds and the pod). Put the rosemary, vanilla bean and seeds, cinnamon stick, peppercorns and citrus zests into a muslin (cheesecloth) bouquet garni bag and secure tightly. Remove the skins from the almonds.

Pour the milk into a paella pan, place the bouquet garni bag in the milk and bring to a boil. Add the rice and almond extract (or a bitter almond, if using), and spread the rice evenly over the bottom of the pan. Reduce the heat to as low as possible. Cook very gently, stirring every 5 minutes, to prevent a skin from forming on the surface. Do not allow it to boil.

After 30 minutes, stir in the sugar until it has dissolved. Add the almonds and stir them into the rice. After another 15 minutes, when the rice has cooked, remove and discard the bag of flavourings. Allow to cool at room temperature. Just before serving, slice the strawberries and arrange them all over the surface of the rice, as if for a tart topping.

SWEET PAELLA RICE WITH FRESH AND DRIED FRUIT

Serves 6
Preparation time: 20 minutes
Cooking time: 45 minutes

3 dried figs

1 banana

1 pear, preferably Williams or Bartlett

1 dessert apple

1 lemon

1 vanilla bean

1 orange

50 g (4 tablespoons) butter

1 tablespoon sultanas (golden raisins)

1½ tablespoons seeded
Muscatel raisins

30 g (3 tablespoons) pitted prunes

20 g (3 tablespoons) dried apricots

3 pitted dates

1 cinnamon stick

2 star anise

50 g (scant ¼ cup) caster (superfine)
sugar

100 g (generous ¼ cup) runny honey

500 ml (2¼ cups) full-fat (whole) milk

200 ml (scant 1 cup) crème fraîche

150 g (¾ cup) short-grain pudding
(pearl) rice

¼ teaspoon saffron threads, toasted
and pounded

To decorate

25 g (¼ cup) caramelized almonds

30 g (¼ cup) caramelized pine nuts

10 large raspberries

20 g (¼ cup) wild strawberries

20 g (scant 1 oz) sloe or damson plums

20 g (1½ tablespoons) blackberries

This dessert works very well with lime or mandarin sorbet to add a touch of acidity. Use a 34-cm (13½-inch) stainless steel or enamelled paella pan.

Cut each dried fig into three pieces. Slice the banana into rounds. Peel, core and cut the pear and the apple into 2-cm (¾-inch) dice. Peel the zest from the lemon with a vegetable peeler, without taking any of the white pith. Split the vanilla bean open along its length and scrape out the seeds with the tip of a sharp knife (reserve the seeds and the pod). Peel the orange in the same way as the lemon, then cut off all the pith and outer membrane from the orange with a serrated knife and extract all the segments.

Melt the butter in a paella pan. Add the diced apple and pear, all the dried fruits, reserved citrus zests, vanilla bean and seeds, cinnamon stick and star anise. Sauté until lightly browned, gently stirring with a wooden spatula. Sprinkle over the sugar and drizzle in the honey, and continue cooking until the sugar has dissolved and caramelized lightly. Add the banana to the pan and cook very briefly.

Pour over the milk, add the crème fraîche and carefully stir the contents of the pan to mix evenly. Bring to a boil and add the rice. Stir through, then return the milk to a boil. Reduce the heat to very low and set the timer to 45 minutes. Make sure that the milk does not come to a boil again during the cooking process, and use a wooden spatula to stir the paella thoroughly every 5 minutes to prevent a skin from forming on the surface.

After 45 minutes the rice should be completely cooked through. Add the saffron, remove the pan from the heat and allow to cool at room temperature. Once the rice has cooled completely, cover the paella with clingfilm (plastic wrap), making sure that this makes contact with the entire surface. Chill in the refrigerator until needed. Just before serving, decorate the top of the paella with the reserved orange segments, raspberries, strawberries, plums, blackberries and caramelized almonds and pine nuts.

GREEN TEA-SCENTED SWEET PAELLA RICE WITH RED BEANS

Serves 6
Preparation time: 15 minutes
Cooking time: 45 minutes

2 teaspoons loose Chinese green tea or 1 green tea bag

4 white cardamom pods

1 star anise

6 coriander seeds

150 g (¾ cup) short-grain pudding (pearl) rice

600 ml (2½ cups) full-fat (whole) milk

100 g (½ cup) caster (superfine) sugar, plus extra, to taste

2 tablespoons matcha (Japanese powdered green tea), to decorate, plus ¼ teaspoon extra, to flavour the rice

125 g (scant ½ cup) well-drained canned adzuki beans

I highly recommend serving this dessert with Japanese-style green tea. Use a 34-cm (13½-inch) stainless steel or enamelled paella pan.

If using loose green tea, tip into a muslin (cheesecloth) bouquet garni bag and secure tightly. Put the cardamom pods, star anise and coriander seeds into a separate bouquet garni bag and tie off securely to seal the spices inside.

Heat 600 ml (2½ cups) water in a paella pan. Just before it comes to a boil, remove the pan from the heat and add the green tea and bouquet garni bag of spices. Allow to infuse for 5 minutes, then remove the green tea bag, leaving the bag of spices in the water in the pan.

Re-heat the infused water to just below boiling point. Add the rice, spreading it evenly over the bottom of the pan, and let cook over very low heat at the slowest possible simmer; do not allow to boil. If you have a timer, set it to 45 minutes.

After 10 minutes, bring the milk to a boil in a separate pan. Stir in the sugar and ¼ teaspoon matcha. Continue stirring until both these ingredients have dissolved, then carefully pour the contents of the pan into the paella pan. After another 10 minutes, add the drained adzuki beans. Remove and discard the bag of spices. Taste, adding a little extra sugar if desired.

Keep checking the progress of the rice at frequent intervals, adding more water if needed. After another 25 minutes, the rice should be cooked: it should be tender but still firm to the bite. Remove the pan from the heat and allow to cool at room temperature. Once the rice has cooled completely, transfer the paella pan to the refrigerator and chill until needed. Just before serving, using a very fine-mesh sieve, sprinkle the matcha over the entire surface of the paella to decorate.

ASTURIAN-STYLE SWEET PAELLA RICE WITH PINEAPPLE

Serves 6
Preparation time: 20 minutes
Cooking time: 45 minutes

1 vanilla bean

4 teaspoons butter

400 g (2½ cups) fresh pineapple, cut into 1.5-cm (¾-inch) cubes

1.3 litres (5½ cups) full-fat (whole) milk

60 ml (¼ cup) anisette liqueur

2 star anise

1 cinnamon stick

zest of lemon, peeled in strips (use a vegetable peeler and avoid any white pith)

2 tablespoons sultanas (golden raisins), or ordinary raisins

175 g (scant 1 cup) short-grain pudding (pearl) rice

100 g (½ cup) caster (superfine) sugar

2½ tablespoons runny honey

50 g (¼ cup) dried haricot (navy) beans, cooked without salt and drained

50 g (¼ cup) raw sugar

A glass of chilled extra-dry cider goes very well with this paella. Use a 34-cm (13½-inch) stainless steel or enamelled paella pan.

Split the vanilla bean along its length and scrape out the seeds with the tip of a pointed knife (set aside the seeds and the pod). Melt the butter in a paella pan and sauté the pineapple cubes. When they start to brown, remove from the pan and set aside. Pour the milk and anisette liqueur into the paella pan. Add the vanilla seeds and bean, star anise, cinnamon, lemon zest and sultanas or raisins. Bring to a boil.

Add the rice, spreading it evenly over the bottom of the pan, and cook over very low heat at the slowest possible simmer. If you have a timer, set it for 45 minutes. Do not allow the milk to boil again during the cooking process, and use a wooden spatula to stir the paella thoroughly every 5 minutes, to prevent a skin from forming on the surface.

After 30 minutes, add the caster (superfine) sugar and honey. Stir thoroughly to dissolve the sugar before adding the haricot (navy) beans.

Cook for another 15 minutes, at which point the rice should be cooked. Add the reserved pineapple and stir through. Remove and discard the lemon zest, cinnamon stick and vanilla bean. Allow to cool at room temperature. Once the rice is barely warm, transfer the paella pan to the refrigerator and chill until needed.

Just before serving, remove the paella from the refrigerator and sprinkle the raw sugar evenly all over the surface of the rice. Use a small chef's blowtorch to caramelize the layer of sugar until evenly glazed and lightly browned.

SWEET PAELLA RICE WITH MANGO AND COCONUT

Serves 6
Preparation time: 15 minutes
Cooking time: 45 minutes

1 lemongrass stalk, tough outer layers removed, cut into very thin rounds

6 fresh lemon verbena leaves

6 fresh lemon balm leaves

6 fresh mint leaves

900 ml (4 cups) full-fat (whole) milk

400 ml (1¾ cups) coconut milk

175 g (scant 1 cup) short-grain pudding (pearl) rice

150 g (¾ cup) caster (superfine) sugar

finely grated zest of 1 lime

3 passion fruit

2 tablespoons butter

400 g (2½ cups) fresh mango cut into 1.5-cm (½-inch) cubes

To decorate

handful of raspberries

mint leaves

sifted icing (confectioners') sugar

Fruit sorbets (lemon, raspberry or mango, to name but a few) go very well with this pudding, and so does a Moscatel dessert wine, which would be my choice to accompany it. Use a 34-cm (13½-inch) stainless steel or enamelled paella pan.

Put the lemongrass, lemon verbena, lemon balm and mint into a small muslin (cheesecloth) bouquet garni bag and secure tightly. Pour the milk and coconut milk into a paella pan. Add the bouquet garni bag of flavourings and bring to a boil. Reduce the heat to very low and add the rice, spreading it evenly over the bottom of the pan. Add the sugar and stir through. Sprinkle over the lime zest, allowing it to fall all over the surface of the rice. If you have a timer, set for 45 minutes. Continue cooking over very low heat, stirring every 5 minutes to prevent a skin from forming on the surface, until the rice is cooked.

After 30 minutes, cut the passion fruit in half crosswise, scoop out the juicy pulp and seeds with a small, sharp-edged teaspoon and add the pulp, seeds and any juices to the paella pan. Remove the bag of flavourings. After another 15 minutes, by which time the rice should be cooked, remove the pan from the heat and set aside.

Melt the butter in a clean pan and gently sauté the mango cubes until they have browned lightly. Stir them thoroughly into the cooked rice. Allow to cool at room temperature until lukewarm. Cover the surface of the rice with clingfilm (plastic wrap), and chill in the refrigerator until needed.

Just before serving, decorate the top of the paella with raspberries and fresh mint leaves, and dust all over with sifted icing (confectioners') sugar.

TAPIOCA DULCE EN PAELLA CON CEREZAS
SWEET TAPIOCA PAELLA WITH CHERRIES

Serves 6
Preparation time: 20 minutes +
15 minutes for soaking
Cooking time: 30 minutes

100 g (⅔ cup) tapioca pearls

2½ tablespoons runny honey

50 g (¼ cup) caster (superfine) sugar

50 ml (¼ cup) cherry syrup (drained from a gently warmed jar of cherry jam or jelly)

2 bananas, sliced into rounds

juice of 1 orange

finely grated zest and juice of 1 lime

100 g (scant ½ cup) crème fraîche

150 g (⅔ cup) very cold whipping cream

50 g (½ cup) caramelized almonds

2 tablespoons caramelized pine nuts

bottled or preserved cherries, to serve

A small glass of sweet wine from Malaga is good with this dessert. Use a 34-cm (13½-inch) stainless steel or enamelled paella pan.

Rinse the tapioca pearls under cold running water, then soak in a bowl of cold water for 15 minutes. Drain. Put the tapioca in a pan, cover with fresh cold water and bring to a boil. Remove from the heat immediately, drain the tapioca and allow to cool. Repeat this process three times, but at the last repetition boil the tapioca until it is very nearly cooked. (Check by examining a tapioca pearl closely. If you can still see a tiny white dot in the centre, but the rest of the pearl is tender and transparent, it is ready.) Tip the tapioca into a fine-mesh sieve. Allow to drain well, then rinse thoroughly under running cold water while you stir the tapioca with your fingertips to keep all the pearls separate. Let drain completely.

Put the honey, sugar and cherry syrup in a paella pan, and cook over medium-high heat until the sugar has dissolved and the mixture has lightly caramelized. Add the banana rounds to the pan with the citrus juices and lime zest. Stir through. Add the tapioca and stir with a wooden spatula for 1 minute. Pour in the crème fraîche and stir. Bring to a boil, and cook over medium heat for 5 minutes, then allow to cool at room temperature.

Meanwhile, whisk the cream until it is thick and greatly increased in volume. Once the tapioca has cooled to lukewarm, using a rubber spatula, fold the whipped cream gently but very thoroughly into the tapioca in the pan. When the mixture is evenly mixed, smooth the surface with the spatula. Cover with clingfilm (plastic wrap) and chill in the refrigerator until needed.

Just before serving, sprinkle the caramelized nuts over the top of the tapioca. Pass around a bowl of preserved cherries separately.

SWEET PAELLA RICE WITH GOAT'S MILK, RHUBARB AND GOAT'S CHEESE

Serves 6
Preparation time: 20 minutes +
6 hours for macerating
Cooking time: 45 minutes

1 lemon

300 g (2½ cups) pink rhubarb, trimmed and cut into 3-cm (1¼-inch) lengths

100 g (½ cup) caster (superfine) sugar

700 ml (scant 3 cups) goat's milk

2 teaspoons sultanas (golden raisins)

150 g (¾ cup) short-grain pudding (pearl) rice

2 small very fresh soft goat's cheese crottins, about 50 g (2 oz) each

100 g (scant ½ cup) preserved cherries, to decorate

I suggest serving walnuts and a very thick compote of raspberries or cherries with this paella, along with a glass of Chablis. Use a 34-cm (13½-inch) stainless steel or enamelled paella pan.

Use a vegetable peeler to remove the zest from the lemon without including any of the white pith. Put the rhubarb and lemon zest in a non-reactive bowl. Add the sugar, mix through and let macerate for 6 hours, stirring occasionally. The sugar will draw out the moisture from the rhubarb stems to form a syrup.

Pour the goat's milk into a paella pan. Add the lemon zest and sultanas (golden raisins), and bring almost to a boil. Add the rice, spreading it evenly over the bottom of the pan, and reduce the heat to as low as possible. If you have a timer, set for 45 minutes and continue cooking very gently. Do not allow to boil.

After 20 minutes, cut both goat's cheeses in half, so that you have 4 fairly thin rounds of cheese. Add to the pan, and stir gently for 5 minutes. Drain the rhubarb, reserving the syrup, and add to the pan, stirring until thoroughly mixed through. After another 20 minutes, when the rice is almost cooked, stir in the reserved sugar syrup. Remove and discard the lemon zest, and distribute the pieces of rhubarb and sultanas as evenly as possible through the rice.

When the rice is cooked, remove the pan from the heat and allow to cool at room temperature. Cover with clingfilm (plastic wrap), making sure it is in direct contact with the entire surface of the rice. Transfer the paella pan to the refrigerator and chill until needed. Just before serving, decorate the top of the paella with the preserved cherries.

SWEET PAELLA RICE WITH APPLES AND CAMEMBERT

Serves 6
Preparation time: 15 minutes
Cooking time: 45 minutes

1 orange

1 cinnamon stick

7 white cardamom pods

2 star anise

2 Orange Reinette, Cox's Orange Pippin
or Cox apples

2 tablespoons unsalted butter

100 ml (scant ½ cup) Calvados
apple brandy

1.6 litres (6¾ cups) full-fat (whole) milk

175 g (scant 1 cup) short-grain pudding
(pearl) rice

2 teaspoons raisins

200 g (1 cup) caster (superfine) sugar

½ round Camembert cheese

ground cinnamon, to serve

1×200-g (7-oz) jar piquillo pepper
preserve (available in specialist
grocery shops, gourmet food stores
and online), to serve

The ports of Brittany, in northern France, were for many years among Europe's main points of entry for spices from the New World. Breton products and culinary techniques, notably that region's traditional oven-baked rice pudding, were the inspiration for this sweet paella.

Use a 34-cm (13½-inch) stainless steel or enamelled paella pan.

Pare off the zest of the orange with a vegetable peeler, leaving behind the bitter white pith. Put the orange zest, cinnamon, cardamom pods and star anise into a muslin (cheesecloth) bouquet garni bag and tie the bag securely. Set aside.

Peel, core and slice the apples thinly. Melt the butter in a paella pan over medium heat. Add the apple slices and sauté until lightly browned and half cooked. Pour over the Calvados and stir, scraping the bottom of the pan with a wooden spatula to deglaze. Add the milk to the pan before the liquid has reduced and darkened too much, and bring to a boil. Now add the rice, bouquet garni bag and raisins. Stir in the sugar and reduce the heat to as low as possible. Cook very gently, stirring every 5 minutes, and do not allow to boil.

After 30 minutes, spread out all the ingredients evenly in the paella pan, and carefully place the Camembert in the centre of the paella. Cook for another 15 minutes.

Once the rice is cooked, remove from the heat and allow to cool at room temperature. Cover with clingfilm (plastic wrap) and chill in the refrigerator until needed. Remove the paella from the refrigerator 1 hour before serving. Using a fine-mesh sieve, lightly dust all over with a little cinnamon. Serve with piquillo pepper preserve.

GLOSSARY

A BANDA   Literally meaning 'next to', the term *a banda* means a dish in which the seafood and fish used to make the stock for the paella are served separately while the paella rice cooks.

ADZUKI BEANS   Small red beans widely used in Japanese cookery, particularly in sweet preparations. They are tender in texture and have a mild, sweet taste.

AIOLI   A Spanish sauce made from garlic and oil, similar to the French *aioli* (garlic mayonnaise), but without the use of eggs.

BLACK SPAGHETTI   Spaghetti made with squid or cuttlefish ink to colour it black.

BLANCH   To plunge food briefly into boiling water to part-cook or remove strong flavours, salt or bitterness before further cooking; also to facilitate the removal of skins or shells.

BOMBA RICE   See Paella rice.

CALASPARRA RICE   A variety of Bomba rice. See Paella rice.

BOTTARGA   The pressed and cured roe of the grey mullet, which is highly prized in Sardinia.

BULGUR WHEAT   A type of wheat that has been soaked, cooked and dried before the bran is removed.

CHINOIS   A conical fine-mesh metal sieve.

CHORIZO   A type of Spanish sausage. It is made with pork and flavoured with smoked paprika. There are two main types: an air-dried sausage that is eaten raw, and smaller fresh sausages which must be cooked before eating.

CHAYOTE   A pale green, furrowed, pear-shaped fruit with cucumber-like flesh surrounding a single seed. It is also known as a christophine, mirliton, cho cho and vegetable pear.

DEGLAZE   To pour a liquid, such as wine, stock or water into a pan in which meat or vegetables have been cooked, in order to dissolve into the sauce any sediments that have stuck to the base of the pan.

FIDEUÁ   A type of dish similar to paella, which is made with noodles, spaghetti bowls, shells or *fideos* (small tubular pasta). It is usually cooked with fish or seafood.

FUMET   A concentrated aromatic stock, usually made from fish but sometimes from poultry, which is used to flavour other stocks and sauces.

HARISSA   A hot, spicy North African paste made with chilli peppers, caraway seeds and herbs.

HON TSUYU   A type of Japanese soup and sauce base made with *dashi* (Japanese stock made with kombu seaweed) and *katsuobushi*.

JAPANESE EEL SAUCE (UNAGI KABAYAKI NO TARE)   A sweet soy-based sauce served with eel in Japanese cuisine.

KATSUOBUSHI   Dried, smoked and fermented Japanese bonito flakes.

LEMON BALM   A type of herb with leaves that have a sweet taste and delicate lemon scent.

LEMON VERBENA   A small shrub with long yellow-green leaves. It has a lemon scent and flavour. The leaves can be used in drinks, salads, fruit dishes and desserts.

MATCHA   A finely powdered green tea used in Japanese cuisine.

MERGUEZ   A type of beef sausage from North Africa. Merguez are heavily spiced with harissa (see above), which gives them their characteristic hot flavour and red colour.

MICROPLANE   A very sharp hand-held grater.

MIRIN   A sweet rice wine, which is used in Japanese cooking.

MORCILLA   A Spanish blood sausage (black pudding), which varies from region to region. Several different flavourings can be used, such as onion or paprika.

NAM PRIK PAO   A type of Thai chilli paste, which is available in Asian grocery stores.

ÑORA PEPPERS   A type of small round red bell pepper with an intense, sweet and pungent flavour. It is always used dried and adds flavour to stews, rice dishes and soups.

PAELLA RICE   A type of round or short-grain rice used specifically for paella. The most famous Spanish variety is bomba, and some of the best bomba rice comes from Calasparra in southeast Spain. Paella rice has a high starch content, so it sticks together somewhat, but the grains can still be easily separated. The grains have the ability to absorb liquid (and therefore flavour) without the structure of the grain breaking down. The central core of the rice grain remains firm, but tender.

PASTIS   A liqueur flavoured with aniseed, which is popular in France.

PICADA   A mixture of almonds, dried fruit and bread pounded in a mortar with garlic and oil. This preparation is often used to thicken sauces and casseroles in Catalonia.

PIMENTÓN   A Spanish variety of paprika, made from red peppers of several varieties. It is almost sweet in taste and is used as a spice. It is added to seafood, sausages, rice and many other savoury dishes. The three main types of *pimentón* are *dulce* (mild or sweet), *agridulce* (bittersweet) and *picante* (hot).

PIQUILLO PEPPERS   A small, red, conical shaped pepper with a sweet flavour, which is grown in Navarra, northern Spain. They are usually available in cans.

PIQUILLO PEPPER PRESERVE   A jam-like preserve made from Piquillo peppers.

QUINOA   A small round grain native to the Andean region of Central America. When cooked, it has a light, fluffy texture and a delicate nutty flavour.

RAS-EL-HANOUT   A North African blend of spices, which typically includes cinnamon, cloves, cumin, fenugreek, fennel seeds, mustard seeds and coriander seeds.

SOBRASADA   A soft, Spanish cured pork sausage flavoured with paprika and herbs.

SOCARRET   A thin layer or crust of crisp rice that forms underneath the cooked rice of a paella.

SOFRITO   An aromatic preparation, which is fundamental to a wide range of Spanish savoury dishes. It often includes chopped onion, paprika, tomato as well as other ingredients.

TAMARIND   A tart fruit from the tamarind tree, used as a spice and souring agent. The fruit contains a sour pulp with many seeds. The pulp can be pressed to form a cake or processed to make a paste.

TAPIOCA   A product of the cassava plant. Cassava flour is treated in such a way as to form flakes, seeds, and pearl tapioca. Pearl tapioca is best for making tapioca pudding.

WILD STRAWBERRIES   A type of strawberry that grows in the wild. They are not cultivated commercially because of their small fruits and low yield, but they are often very delicious.

DIRECTORY

The following stores stock high quality Spanish products such as paella rice, Serrano ham, olive oil, cheese and other items used in these recipes.

UNITED STATES

EAST COAST

Despaña
408 Broome Street
New York, NY 10013
+1 212 219 5050
www.despananyc.com

SOUTH EAST

A Southern Season
201 S. Estes Drive
University Mall
Chapel Hill, NC 27514
+1 800 253 3663
www.southernseason.com

La Tienda
1325 Jamestown Road
Williamsburg, VA 23185
+1 888 331 4362
www.latienda.com

MIDWEST

Zingerman's
422 Detroit Street
Ann Arbor, MI 48104
+1 888 636 8162
www.zingermans.com

WEST COAST

La Española Meats, Inc.
25020 Doble Avenue
Harbor City, CA 90710
+1 310 539 0455
www.laespanolameats.com

The Spanish Table
(4 locations)
1426 Western Avenue
Seattle, WA 98101
+1 206 682 2827

1814 San Pablo Avenue
Berkeley, CA 94702
+1 510 548 1383

800 Redwood Highway 123
Mill Valley, CA 94941
+1 415 388 5043

109 N Guadalupe Street
Santa Fe, NM 87501
+1 505 986 0243
www.spanishtable.com

CANADA

Pasquale Bros. Downtown Ltd.
16 Goodrich Road
Etobicoke, Ontario M8Z 4Z8
+1 416 364 7397
www.pasqualebros.com

UNITED KINGDOM

LONDON

Bayley & Sage
60 High Street
Wimbledon Village
London SW19 5EE
+44 (0)20 8946 9904

Brindisa
The Floral Hall
Borough Market, Stoney Street
London SE1 9AF
+44 (0)20 7407 1036
www.brindisa.com

East Dulwich Deli
15–17 Lordship Lane
London SE22 8EW
+44 (0)20 8693 2525
www.eastdulwichdeli.com

Iberica
195 Great Portland Street
London W1W 5PS
+44 (0)20 7636 8650
www.ibericalondon.co.uk

R Garcia & Sons
248–250 Portobello Road
London W11 1LL
+44 (0)20 7221 6119
www.garciacafe.co.uk

Raoul's Deli
8–10 Clifton Road
London W9 1SZ
+44 (0)20 7289 6649
www.raoulsgourmet.com

THE SOUTH

Williams & Brown
28a Harbour Street, Whitstable
Kent CT5 1AH
+44 (0)1227 274 507

Chandos Deli
6 Princess Victoria Street, Clifton
Bristol BS8 4BP
+44 (0)1179 743 275
www.chandosdeli.com

Effings
50 Fore Street, Totnes
Devon TQ9 5RP
+44 (0)1803 863435
www.effings.co.uk

THE NORTH

Appleyards
85 Wyle Cop, Shrewsbury
Shropshire SY1 1UT
+44 (0)1743 240 180

Define Food & Wine
Chester Road, Sandiway
Cheshire CW8 2NH
+44 (0)1606 882 101
www.definefoodandwine.com

Roberts & Speight
40 Norwood, Beverley
North Humberside HU17 9EY
+44 (0)1482 870 717
www.hamperbox.co.uk

AUSTRALIA

Delicado Foods
134 Blues Point Road
McMahons Point
Sydney NSW 2060
+61 2 9955 9399
www.delicadofoods.com.au

Casa Iberica
25 Johnston Street
Fitzroy
Melbourne VIC 3065
+61 3 9417 7106
www.casaibericadeli.com.au

Alimento Deli
99 Smith Street
Summer Hill
Sydney NSW 2130
+61 2 9797 2484

El Mercado
72 Tennyson Road
Mortlake
Sydney NSW 2137
+61 2 8757 3700
www.elmercado.com.au

INDEX

THIS BOOK IS DEDICATED TO MY CUSTOMERS, WHO HAVE MADE THIS ADVENTURE POSSIBLE.

AUTHOR'S ACKNOWLEDGEMENTS

To Vanina Herráiz, my wife, for her help, support and patience, and her continual search for perfection, particularly in this book dedicated to paella.

To all the members of the Fogón team, for their collaboration and enthusiasm each and every day, especially in the making of this book.

To Sophie Brissaud, who excels as much in her culinary knowledge as she does in her writing, for her co-operation and *savoir-faire*.

To Jean-Marie del Moral, for his loyal friendship.

To Fernando Gutiérrez, for his inspiration and talent.

To all the members of the Phaidon editorial team who have worked on this project, particularly to Hélène Gallois Montbrun for her patience and efficiency.

To Ramón Chao, a Galician in Paris who has always believed in rice, and who has helped me in my work for more than a decade.

To Jeannine Coureau, our own Carmen of the Île Saint-Louis.

To Juan Mir, the great defender, who never lets a grain of rice slip.

To Pascal Allaman and Marc Vernède, who opened their kitchen to us for some of the photography.

To Oscar Caballero, who upended my notion of Adam and Eve and the forbidden fruit.

To all the food writers who have helped me understand paella, and without whom all this would not have been possible.

To the colleagues whose paths I have crossed since the beginnings of my adventure, and who have given me a lot.

Finally, to Paris, the city that gave me everything, and inspires every cook in the world.

Opposite: Research into paella techniques continually evolving. Here, a paella *a ban* has been returned to the pan after cook to create a crisp, uniform textu

RECIPE NOTES

Unless otherwise stated, milk is assumed to be whole.

Unless otherwise stated, eggs are assumed to be large and individual vegetables and fruits, such as onions and apples, are assumed to be medium.

Unless otherwise stated, all herbs are fresh.

Unless otherwise stated, pepper is freshly ground black pepper.

Cooking times are for guidance only, as individual ovens and stoves vary. If using a fan oven, follow the manufacturer's instructions concerning oven temperatures.

To test whether your deep-frying oil is hot enough, add a cube of stale bread. If it browns in 30 seconds, the temperature is 350–375°F (180–190°C), about right for most frying. Exercise caution when deep frying. Wear long sleeves and never leave the pan unattended.

Some recipes include raw or very lightly cooked eggs, meat or fish. These should be avoided by the elderly, infants, pregnant women, convalescents and anyone with an impaired immune system.

Cup and metric measures are given throughout. Follow one set of measurements, not a mixture, as they are not interchangeable.

All cup and spoon measurements are level. 1 cup = 8 fl oz; 1 teaspoon = 5 ml; 1 tablespoon = 15 ml. Australian standard tablespoons are 20 ml, so Australian readers are advised to use 3 teaspoons in place of 1 tablespoon when measuring small quantities.

Phaidon Press Limited
Regent's Wharf
All Saints Street
London N1 9PA

Phaidon Press Inc.
180 Varick Street
New York, NY 10014

www.phaidon.com

First published 2011
© 2011 Phaidon Press Limited
ISBN 978 0 7148 6082 4

A CIP catalogue record for this book is available from the British Library.

Designed by
Studio Fernando Gutiérrez
Introduction text and recipe editing by Sophie Brissaud
Photographs by Jean-Marie del Moral, except page 4 (Pablo Picasso having dinner with friends, 1947), akg-images/Denise Bellon; page 34 (Central Market, Valencia, Spain), Photolibrary.com; page 130 (Almonte, Spain), akg-images/PictureContact; page 160 (La Pepica restaurant, Valencia, Spain), Richard Schlagman; page 176 (fruit stall in Barcelona, Spain), Vincent Liu.

Printed in China